Angela McGerr

The ANGEL QUEST of the HEART

A journey of spiritual transformation

Illustrations by Richard Rockwood

Quadrille

Angela's Quest

About the quest ❧

The Way of Love and Light is the Way of Divine Truth. It has many paths, some straight and some circuitous, but all lead to One; and One leads to All. This quest is Melchisadec's Rainbow Path of the Heart and it is found first through his Sacred Seven: Hope, Courage, Truth, Wisdom, Beauty, Harmony and Healing. Hermes Trismegistos adds three more to fulfil his Law of Three: for Magic and Transformation lead to Tranquillity. Seven times three equals twenty-one – still three, but seven plus three makes ten, the One Truth of All held in the Sacred Eight of Eternity; the Key of which resides within the Chalice of your Heart.

This is the story of a life-changing quest, and I have termed it *The Angel Quest of the Heart*. The reason for this is that the open (higher) heart is the key to All. This quest takes you along the infinite and eternal Way of Love and Light, the Way of the angels leading to inner peace. As I wrote in my first book, *A Harmony of Angels*, this Way involves Sacred Seven: Hope, Courage, Truth, Wisdom, Beauty, Harmony and Healing, as well as Sacred Three: Magic, Transformation and Tranquillity. By choosing to commence the quest you will gradually build all these special qualities within yourself. If you complete the quest the angels will help you finally to reach a level of vibration that heals and opens the flower in the very heart of your heart, creating that place of inner peace – connection to All – that we seek.

You can follow the complete quest once or up to seven times, on each occasion achieving a different level of healing in mind, body and spirit. Every time you do the quest there will be further transformation in lower self, your heart will open further and you will grow spiritually through higher self, your own level of vibration becoming ever more finely tuned. First, you work to heal self and life through Melchisadec's basic rainbow colours, but then, as you re-do the quest, each colour will become gradually paler as its (and your) vibration rises. There are at least seven levels of colour vibration as the angels instruct you further and you achieve a new, higher level of spiritual consciousness, drawing ever nearer to the vibration of the angels themselves. As you choose a life filled with angels every day they rejoice as they enfold you in unconditional love.

Although you cannot do the quest for others, by finding this spiritual peace within yourself you will begin to radiate this tranquillity into your aura and beyond. For although it is impossible to live an entirely stress-free life, you can learn the secret of the labyrinth: how Love and Light can open the flower of your higher heart. As the resulting inner peace flows out from you, the dynamic around you changes to reflect your heart's new tranquillity, thus changing the atmosphere around you. Not only will this aid others to feel less stressed, but they will also want some of what you have found, and so their own Angel Quest of the Heart may begin. In effect, you will have shown them the Way. Then the choice is theirs.

IS THERE A CATCH? There is no catch at all, except I must point out that, as the saying goes, nothing is entirely free in this world. We all know folks who are 'spiritual shoppers', hoping to find total inner peace through a one-day workshop. You cannot achieve true transformation without some kind of firm commitment to change. Otherwise, deep down inside you do not really want it. In the case of the quest, you are committing to working on healing mind, body and spirit with the angels and their unconditional love, and to growing spiritually on the Way of Love and Light.

HOW DOES IT WORK? This quest is my personal story of self-healing and spiritual awareness, but it can be your story, too. It is the quest of the mighty angel Melchisadec, Father to the Sacred Seven Angels of our Solar System. Also of Hermes Trismegistos, the alchemist, and his Law of Three; of the Elemental Angels who help govern our life; and finally of Pistis Sophia, the Heavenly Mother of the Star Angels and Guardian of Eight and Eternal Wisdom. All will become clear in due course, but first, ask yourself some questions.

Is there something missing from your life? Is your purse full but your spirit parched? Are you going through the motions of life, busy and stressed, but feeling that there must be something more than what you see around you? Have you found any white feathers lately (a spiritual sign from the angels)? If you have, read on, and if you haven't, well you soon will. Finally: is your true heart's desire to find inner peace?

I, too, was once like this, but now with the help of the angels I have found that tranquillity. So I offer you this quest – a spiritual consciousness-raising experience that enables you to find this peace in the heart of your own heart.

When I was in that fraught situation, I wondered what I could do to help heal myself. I was not alone, because I knew I could invoke the angels to advise me. How? Well, those of you who have read my books will know that to invoke the power of an angel, you first use the angel's sacred name, then speak from your heart, and finally use the forces of Love and Light. You will call in the angelic vibration to lift and enfold you towards your Divine self. And this is just the start.

For Pistis Sophia advises you that Love is the key to overcoming adversity to rewrite the template of your life in her Stars. Hermes Trismegistos proclaims that Wisdom comes from Power used only with Love. And Melchisadec urges you on, saying that now is your time of true spiritual awakening, of fast-tracking your soul journey on the Way of Love and Light. If this resonates, then Melchisadec's power of Sacred Seven and his labyrinth await you, likewise Hermes Trismegistos' Three Paths of the Soul. Discover how angels, colours, mysteries and secrets join and coalesce, as you use this new-found awareness to gradually heal and harmonise yourself, finally arriving at the heart of your heart where Pistis Sophia awaits. However, the Spiritual Laws say that to give is to receive. The angels require you to make a vow – and this is most important – that when you reach this place of peace and find bliss, you pledge to return and show others the Way.

How it all began ❧

Seven are the Mansions of the House of the Mighty. Three are the Paths of the Soul: Man, Liberty, and Light (from the Emerald Tablets of Thoth/Hermes Trismegistos, Doreal translation)

One Saturday in 1999 I was feeling drained and tired after a hard week. I'd had a successful business for seven years, had money to spend, a good marriage and lovely children, but for some inexplicable reason I was no longer completely satisfied. I didn't even know what I didn't know... I just knew there was something indefinable missing in my life.

I sensed things were about to change, although I had no idea what was in store. I'd embarked on learning healing and been taught that angels would come if invited – at the time I found this concept difficult to accept. I'd also been told that guidance would come in meditation. On the spur of the moment I decided to do a form of meditation in which I lay on the bed, closed my eyes and invoked angels from my heart to help me to find what I was seeking. I knew that first of all (as I later wrote in A *Harmony of Angels*) I needed to follow Thoth/Hermes Trismegistos' Sacred Law of Three, to manifest the angel energy around me.

From my heart and with honest intent, I invoked Michael for protection and truth, Haniel for love and beauty, and Cassiel, ruler of the day – Saturday – to be with me in Love and Light, Love and Light, Love and Light. (Later I was to discover that I was born on a Saturday, so Cassiel will always be special to me.) Feeling tingling and warmth on my hands signifying the angels' presence, I started taking some deep breaths of pure, white Light, also known as Spiritus Dei, the breath of The Creator, the very energy from which the angels are formed. With angelic help I breathed in the positive, white Light energy, and breathed out my frustrations, my fatigue, dissatisfaction – all the negative energy I could think of – until presently I had let go of that dark energy and I felt I was becoming filled to overflowing with pure crystalline Angelic Light.

Then, from my heart I connected through my feet to Mother Earth, and with Love I sent this Light to join with the atoma (blue-crystalline sun) at her heart, feeling it curling around and into this sphere. As Mother Earth sent me back blue-violet light, I brought this through me and breathed it out around me, gradually forming a tunnel, fashioned of spirals of white and sapphire Light, that stretched before me across time and space.

Finally, knowing that my physical self was under the protection of Michael, the divine essence that was my spirit travelled with Haniel and Cassiel through the tunnel of Light until the sky-blue circle that was the end of the tunnel drew nearer. Presently, I emerged and found myself in bright sunshine, near the top of a mountain. Its peak was directly above me. The air was pure and clear, yet the summit had a swirling golden cloud around it almost as if it was crowned in light. A voice addressed me: "We three are the Guardian Angels of the True Self, of Mountains and of Time itself. Can you name us?" As I gave the three names, the first angel spoke again: "I welcome you to this point. Your first task is to commit to reaching the summit of my Sacred Mountain, for to find the heart of your heart takes time and effort. From there you can choose to continue to the start of the quest itself."

I could not see a proper path and it all seemed very rocky and forbidding. I have never been a very outdoor person. Should I bother with this? I hesitated and mentally asked for support, and then I heard a baying, and a magnificent hound appeared, with a glossy rose-gold coat. He carried a rucksack in his jaws that he dropped on the ground at my feet. "I am the Hound of Heaven, a Mystical Animal Guide", he informed me. "Like all my kind I provide a bridge between the earthly, devic and angelic realms. My own specific purpose is to be your faithful friend, to be there whenever you need me, and yet to reflect to you both positive and negative aspects of yourself – things you need to change but do not always want to recognise in yourself. What do you see in my eyes now?"

I looked deep into the Hound's golden eyes, and in their reflection I saw intelligence and flexibility, but also a lack of stamina at times, a superficial side of my character that I did not want to see, such as a desire for quick solutions. I heard myself say that I didn't know if I could summon the energy to climb this steep mountain to find true self and inner peace, as I could not even see the path. The Hound sensed my hesitation, and looked at me now with eyes full of love and compassion. "Do not be weighed down with difficulties and reasons not to try. Pick up my gift of a rucksack, follow me and I will show you how to reach the peak."

Sure enough, he disappeared around a rock and, as I followed him, I found it was not hard at all, as once he showed me the path I did not even have to walk. I glided along it, thus soon gaining the summit. "I leave you here for now," he said, "but my gift will help you in due course. When you reach the centre of the labyrinth I shall return."

I looked inside the rucksack; it contained nothing. As I stood on the peak, looking down and wondering what to do next, a large, shining white bird approached me, holding a book in its beak. The bird was a strange mixture of dove and eagle, fierce yet ethereal, strong yet graceful. As the bird perched nearby, it offered me the book. "Who or what are you?" I asked. "I am the Thunderbird," was the reply. "My brief is to guide mankind's spiritual development – I can show you what you will attain with true balance, for when you truly harmonise masculine/feminine mind, body and spirit aspects of self to achieve wholeness then you can become a Thunderbeing. First I will guide you to Templa Mar, the timeless, etheric temple. There, if you so choose, you will commence the walk through Melchisadec's labyrinth to the centre, wherein is found wholeness through healing and opening your higher heart (the heart grail). Then you are on the way to becoming a Thunderbeing. The quest requires the solving of many secrets and mysteries, but all you need to know is contained within this book. However, we ask you to make the necessary time commitment to solve all the riddles. Also, most importantly, when you have gained and opened your heart grail you must pledge to help others find the Way. If you agree to do this, take the book and follow me." I grasped the book and thus, as I placed it in the rucksack, my quest really began.

The Thunderbird swooped elegantly down the path in front of me which wound down the mountainside. Ahead of me in the distance was a wood, starting with a grove of slender larches like arrowheads pointing to the sky, as if to say that the only way was up. There were also regal oaks, ash trees, redwoods and other wise forest sentinels. I glided down the path and soon came to the beginning of the wood. As I looked into the shady interior, I perceived a presence formed of golden light flowing through green leaves and a noble totem within.

"I am Guardian Angel of Trees and therefore of this wood," proclaimed a voice in my heart. "If you can name me, you have permission to connect with the ancient tree energies through mind, body and spirit as you walk through my sacred wood. This strength will aid you to complete the quest." I was able to name this angel, and strength flowed into me. I thanked the angel and proceeded slowly through the wood, feeling its sacredness. I reached out with both hands and spirit to touch and absorb the trees' nurturing energies. I sent them Love and Light and in return they allowed me to draw on their nobility and connect with their firm foundations, from which I vowed that I, too, would reach from the heart of Mother Earth towards the sky and All That Is.

As I half walked, half glided through the trees, I smelled sweetly scented flowers. Achaiah, Guardian Angel of the Secrets of Nature, whispered in my heart that flowers would aid me at various times, and indeed that I should consult my book to identify certain flowers linked to the various chakra energy centres of the body. The quest would offer the opportunity to heal these. Then out of the corner of my eye I glimpsed something gleaming through the trees, a horse-like creature fashioned out of quicksilver interwoven with rose gold, its mane of bright moonbeams. When I tried to focus on it, it seemed to disappear, until suddenly my eyes captured it for an instant – a Unicorn, dazzlingly graceful – and then it was gone and my heart felt bereft. "If you succeed in this quest and fulfil your pledge, you will earn the right to continue and eventually work with the Unicorn," said the voice of Hariel, Guardian Angel of Animals. "For he is the Divine one of the devic kingdom; until then other Mystical Animal Guides or devas will assist your progress."

Suddenly the trees thinned and the sunshine penetrated once more. In front of me was an amazing sight: a huge temple of white marble columns with shining marble and crystal domes. The temple seemed to hover in spirals of white and violet above an emerald mist, reached only by steps made out of Light. The sun glittered on the crystal domes, forming dazzling rainbows in the swirling mists. I suddenly understood what the word 'awe-inspiring' really meant as I viewed its unearthly beauty. "This is Templa Mar, the etheric temple of healing that was, is and ever shall be here for mankind, for those whose hearts are able and willing to connect to it through the Way of Love and Light. I will leave you now for the angels will take over, but I shall see you again", said Thunderbird, as she soared skywards.

Templa Mar ❧

I pledge to show others the Way

It took me several minutes to gain the courage to approach this temple, to make my way to the foot of the Light steps, but a presence awaited me there – a being of glittering geometry surrounded by wing-like light streamers of pink and golden light. "I am Roshel," said a gentle voice in my heart. If you can tell me what my Guardian Angel responsibilities are I will allow you to climb my Ladder of Light to start your spiritual quest." When I replied, she stood aside and gave permission for me to climb. Presently I stood at the top of the ladder, on a platform of Light and before a pair of pillars, one of gold and the other silver. They framed a great oaken gate, embossed with golden suns, silver moons, glittering quartz crystal stars and fleur de lys.

Then a beautiful circular rainbow materialised, within which was a splendid being emanating many different shades of violet Light rays. He held a kind of chalice containing a cross key. "Welcome to Templa Mar and the Way of Love and Light", the words resonated within my head and heart. Next appeared a golden being whose silvery Light wings somehow reminded me of the shape of the fleur de lys on the entrance gate. He was surrounded by a rosy radiance, like rose petals made of living Light, and wore an unusual crown of gold. This second being then addressed me: "Can you name our guardianships," he asked, "and a symbol for each of us? For these are also connected with this quest." As I replied, I remembered reading and memorising some of the cryptic and ancient words in his Emerald Tablets, but at the time, not really understanding them. Then, as if he had read my thoughts (as indeed he probably had) he asked me: "How many mansions or chambers are there within this labyrinth?" "Correct," he replied as I answered. "Now tell me about the Paths of the Soul." "Well remembered!" he exclaimed, on hearing my answer. "You need to know this, for the Labyrinthine Quest of Melchisadec will take you on a triple path through each of these healing mansions, or chambers, as a consequence of which your spiritual consciousness will become mighty indeed," he promised.

"Do you wish to commit to the quest of my seven-turn labyrinth?" invited Melchisadec.

"And through spiritual alchemy transform yourself and your life with my Law of Three?" asked Hermes Trismegistos. "For I have also written that Three is the Mystery come from the Great One."

"What does it all involve?" I cautiously enquired.

"Well," replied Melchisadec, "Templa Mar has many quests. As your Angelic spiritual director I offer you the labyrinthine quest whose objective is to use sacred geometry to open the flower of your heart grail (what is termed your higher heart) through harmonising mind, body and spirit. The labyrinth is Macrocosm: All in Divine Harmony or Oneness. You are Microcosm, striving towards Macrocosm – Oneness with All. To reconcile the two you heal your seven energy centres one at a time in the labyrinth's Sacred Seven Mansions. When all these energy centres (chakras) flow and function more effectively, you can reach the labyrinth's heart where Pistis Sophia, your Heavenly Angel Mother, waits to help you open your own higher heart or eighth chakra, for that brings in inner peace. The point is that any or all of your chakra energy centres may have been either veiled or blocked by life's many challenges. Undertaking the quest to experience and surmount whatever unfolds gives you an opportunity not only to learn more about yourself, but also to remove blocks preventing you from moving on in life. To follow the Law of Three, each mansion has two Guardian Angels and a Mystical Animal Guide, though some do have more; the point is that all these beings are most anxious to support you on the Way."

"Is opening the higher heart how spiritual consciousness is raised?" I ventured to ask.

"Indeed that is a mighty step to Oneness with All, but remember, all through the quest you are actually travelling the Way of Love and Light itself," vouchsafed Hermes Trismegistos. "In fact, as well as your experiences in the seven mansions you visit, each right-angle turn of the labyrinth raises consciousness and is therefore a form of spiritual alchemy. We angels aid you to self-heal and transform, step by step, though of course the real work must be done by you. You also need to use the quest's alchemy to widen your own belief system, and it is that with which we help you most. What I bring you is the knowledge of how strong your own will can be when combined with a heart filled with loving intent. At this point you have no idea of what you can do with that power!"

Melchisadec continued: "To summarise, then, as the quest proceeds through each mansion you revisit your core values, determine mind and body issues to heal and, at the same time, raise your spiritual consciousness. In the seventh mansion I help you ignite your own Angelic Light centre within. Then you are ready for the Place of the Higher Heart, the heart of the labyrinth itself, where Pistis Sophia awaits you. If you succeed in reaching this point you will understand the meaning of my Chalice and Key, for there you will discover your own higher heart or true self. And as Love and Light opens your higher heart flower Pistis Sophia says you can rewrite your life template in the stars. At this point you will have experienced much spiritual alchemy, but you can do the whole quest again – in fact you can do it seven times over – to keep working the alchemy and raising your vibration gradually closer to ours. The closer you get to us, the more we can aid and support you. This is an eternal truth of Templa Mar, the etheric Healing Temple."

Remembering what the Hound of Heaven had reflected back to me, I responded without hesitation: "I commit!" And so the die was cast. "To go through the first archway leading to the labyrinth you must answer riddles of Sacred Seven and Three, but do not be daunted," Melchisadec advised. "Can you answer the following? There are seven colours in the traditional rainbow. Which colour do I rule?" "Correct," he said, as I replied. "Now, name all my Sacred Seven Angels with their seven planetary guardianships. Also, what are the key attributes they bring you for this labyrinthine journey on the Way of Love and Light?"

"Good, good," he commented, on hearing my reply. So these are what I need in the quest I thought to myself, as suddenly the pieces fell into place. Hermes Trismegistos then asked: "Three more are added to the seven, for they bring magical transformation leading to inner peace and tranquillity. Name the three and their planetary guardianships." To my words he replied, "Excellent!" Then continued: "The final question requires you to vouchsafe to us what you will do when you have succeeded in completing the quest – that is to say, found and opened your heart grail."

As I gave the correct answer, Melchisadec and Hermes Trismegistos glided aside and the great gates opened, exposing an archway of white marble blocks. Through this I perceived a beautiful, light-filled courtyard paved with black-and-white tiles in a chessboard pattern and ornamented with pewter planters filled with a variety of fragrant white flowers. I recognised roses, jasmine and orange blossom. An olive tree stood near the entrance. It was all very harmonious. I heard the voice of Melchisadec in my heart: "This courtyard symbolises something you are seeking. If you can answer which of my Sacred Seven angels is represented here, then this angel will appear to take you to the first labyrinthine pathway." As I replied with the correct answer the angel immediately appeared. "You have gained permission to start the quest proper; just follow the corridors," announced my angel guide. He then escorted me down a short corridor and, as I turned a right angle to the left, he dematerialised. My quest was about to begin in earnest.

Chapter 1

Healing Mansion of the Sun
▬ *Ignite Healing Sun within and All becomes possible*

I stood at the beginning of a corridor that curved gently to the right. The roof was made of clear crystal, interspersed with gold calcite, through which the sun's rays danced, causing rainbows to sparkle in the air and striking bright reflected beams from a floor that shone like beaten gold. I followed this corridor for a certain distance, all the while feeling that I was absorbing the light and that it could dispel any darkness within me. Then suddenly, hidden in a sort of deep niche recessed into the wall on the left of the pathway, so that I had not been able to see it before, appeared an archway of yellow granite blocks flecked with black.

Within it was a great gate made of yew wood. The light from the corridor struck clear crystals arranged in a six-pointed star pattern around intricate carvings and embosses, for the gate was embellished with symbols of hidden secrets of healing and alchemy. Far more startling than this, however, was that beside it reclined the Guardian of the Gate – a huge golden lion with vivid blue eyes. He was not exactly solid, nor was he entirely opaque, but he shimmered, rather like the light in the desert that shifts and wavers. The light around him was bright with different shades of gold, as if the sun was in his heart, as no doubt it was. Beneath his right paw protruded what I recognised as an ankh, symbol of eternal life. "Who are you?" I asked anxiously. "I am the Solar Lion, mystical animal deva and emissary of those who are Sun born, that is those who can heal others. Do not be afraid," he reassured me, "for like all devas I am your link to the angelic realm and gatekeeper of this mansion."

"To open this gate you need to answer some questions for me and also to obtain my ankh. Firstly do you know which angel rules here?" As I replied, the Lion continued: "Apart from the ankh, name a flower, a crystal and a symbol of alchemy linked to the Sun Mansion. Then if you tell me the meaning of the ankh, you can acquire it."

I answered all these questions to his satisfaction, so the Lion took the ankh in his great jaws and offered it to me. As I grasped the ankh, for a brief moment I connected directly with the magnificent animal deva and some of his glowing light and warmth passed through the

ankh and into my hand; from there it flowed into my solar plexus – the centre of my will. "Why, I feel something from you!" I cried. "Yes, it's healing energy, and when you have visited this mansion you will be able to feel even more." My confidence in the quest grew. He stood to one side of the gate. As I held the ankh it continued to glow and I peered more closely at the gate's centre. I then perceived that there was in fact a kind of keyhole – an ankh-shaped depression in the gate itself, and on a sudden inspiration I fitted the ankh into this. The gate immediately swung open and I passed through it, feeling quite pleased with myself. The Lion followed me and the gate closed on us both.

We found ourselves in a huge and dazzling circular chamber, carved entirely out of clear quartz crystal. Within it was a four-sided crystal pyramid, its uppermost point directly below the centre of the crystal roof, which had a circular opening to the Sun. I was in the presence of a huge being, with great golden Light wings, radiating crystalline purity. I knew it to be the Ruler of the Sun and patron angel of healing himself. "Welcome," came the words, "to the first stage and highest priority of your life-changing process. You were able to tell my Lion the meaning of the ankh; this is also the purpose of the quest. However, you need to know more about the part the labyrinth plays. To comply with the Law of Three there are three healing aspects within each of the labyrinth's seven paths, that is to say, seven times three, which is twenty-one (and if you add together these two numbers, still therefore three). What are these three aspects?" He asked rhetorically, and continued: "Why, the healing of mind, body and spirit, or lower self, heart and higher self. Which do you think you need?" "I need all three," I replied at once.

He went on: "And then there are seven separate cycles that you can engage in with the labyrinth. My Lion will tell you more. Here, in this chamber, we start the first cycle. You begin to deal with mind, body and spirit – although the quest will also help with your spiritual development, for the more you commit to it, the more you are able to raise your spiritual consciousness."

Hermes Trismegistos then re-materialised, together with a third angel whose wings emanated pale sun-yellow flames. "Now I'd like to introduce Gazardiel," intoned Hermes

Trismegistos. "Under my direction he initiates spiritual alchemy through the healing energy of the Sun, as you will shortly see. To start off the mind healing process," he went on, "focus on the fact that the Sun is life, as well as the centre of all will-power within you, for when you ignite the Sun's positive energy within yourself All becomes possible. You will gain in knowledge and wisdom, enabling you to work your own spiritual alchemy leading towards your reconnection with All. If you can tell me the energy centre that applies here, you can see that I speak only truth." I answered his question immediately. "Enjoy yourself!" proclaimed Hermes Trismegistos, as he nodded and then slowly dematerialised, leaving me in the care of the other angels.

"On a certain level the pyramid is a masculine representation of Sun, Earth and Fire power," the Ruler of the Sun told me as he drew a door on the crystal side of the pyramid, which promptly opened. The angels and the Lion motioned me inside and followed me in, after which the door disappeared again, sealing us in. Then I was directed to a crystal couch in the very centre of the pyramid itself, underneath the uppermost point, and invited to lie down. Although it appeared to be crystal, the couch was not cold and hard but warm and, as I lay down on it, it seemed to mould itself to my body shape. I felt as if I was suspended in living crystal within that sacred pyramid shape, itself within the circular Sun Mansion.

"You see we must address both masculine and feminine aspects of healing. While the geometry of the sphere is broadly feminine and the pyramid masculine, in this duality universe they both have aspects of each other. To heal both these aspects within you, you need to create a Sun sphere within your lower self, but you will also form a pyramid for masculine balance, although this will only become fully functional after you've addressed what you need to heal in the other lower-self mansions of Uranus and Mars/Earth. The sphere holds the potential for Angelic Light within, while the pyramid allows Sun, Earth and Fire energy to flow upwards from lower self (for Fire rises from Earth) to heal the heart.

"Having said that, I might as well add that the Moon energy works the same way in reverse, as you will discover in the Mansion of Moon, Neptune & Water. Committing to healing your heart creates a corresponding overlapping Moon sphere (this forms a vesica

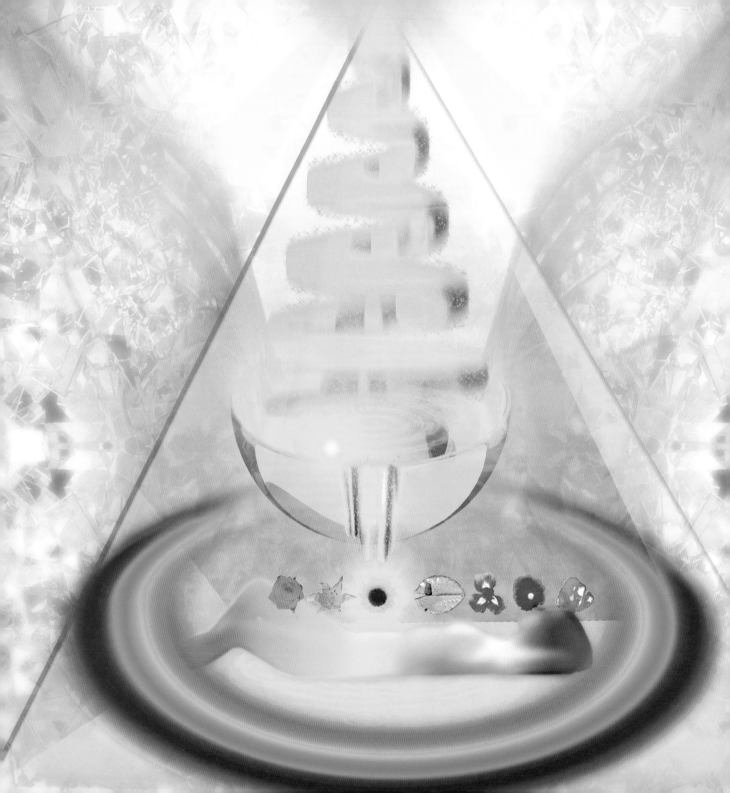

piscis – of which more later on in the quest). Also, you can create a downward-pointing pyramid (for Water falls from Air) within you through which Moon, Air and Water energy healing flow. This is to balance the Sun, Earth and Fire pyramid we create here. When both are fully balanced they form a star, like the one on the gate, except that it is three-dimensional. Still, first things first. You will understand more in due course!" That said, the Ruler of the Sun caused a Light ray to spiral directly down through the roof of the chamber and apex of the crystal pyramid, and Gazardiel held a golden bowl to receive this liquid Sunlight that scintillated as it flowed in a vortex into the bowl. "You see this is the very essence of Light. All you need now is Love, and we provide this for you."

Gazardiel then poured Light from the bowl directly onto that energy centre within me that would start my healing process. As the angels surrounded me with Love, I felt as if a sphere of bright golden Light ignited around my yellow energy centre, a burst of real solar Fire within. "This first step actually empowers your mind, specifically your will and intent, with positive Sun energy," I was told, "for you have no idea how dynamic this can really be."

"Now we move on to start healing the body. What is your focus do you think?" "Well I have been suffering from irritable bowel syndrome for more than ten years, and it has started to rule my life, plus I other have digestive problems." The Lion placed a small quartz crystal pyramid (tetrahedron) upright at the base of my ribcage. Raphael's spiral ray struck the crystal pyramid and a beautiful circular rainbow shimmered over me. As it did so, bright and beautiful flowers – one for each of the seven different rainbow hues – appeared, floating over each relevant energy centre. "See, these are the flowers you were shown by Achaiah," he commented. "They symbolise how the seven main energy centres will appear when fully healed." As I watched, the flowers became translucent, still with colour but rather like a watercolour version instead of a true representation, though some were brighter than others.

"Now, these pale flowers show how your energy centres look at the moment," he advised. "Also, your heart flower only contains green at present, that is leaves and buds, but as we have told you there are really two heart centres. When you have healed the personal heart centre with green, then you will work on what is termed the higher heart. This is the eighth energy centre: the heart of pure love that does not judge. When you begin to feel this emotion then the most beautiful flower of all will appear in full colour in your heart."

"How can I start to heal them, then?" I asked. "First, you need to understand that to be whole in mind, body and spirit you must ultimately take responsibility for yourself," replied the patron angel of healing. "Though others can help, it is the power of your own will and intent that can make all the difference. In this mansion, will your own Sun sphere to aid you to absorb and begin to process each coloured flower," were the next words I heard in my heart. As I did so, the flowers merged into and became part of me. Each energy centre then glowed a little more brightly, although all the flowers were still rather translucent. "Now, in this mansion you focus particularly on the yellow, and in each different mansion work on the specific energy centre involved," he instructed.

And so, using the Sun sphere now within my lower self, I immediately focused my will to radiate Sun energy into the yellow energy centre, to address the digestive and IBS problems. It was amazing – I could actually feel myself being healed in that particular chakra, and the yellow flower pulsed with light. Then both orange and red flowers brightened and became slightly more distinct. I was confident that I had begun a process of healing at a primary level. In fact, with my newly empowered will, I firmly believed that I could continue this healing by constantly replenishing the Sun sphere within self and willing it first to energy centres and then to my very cells themselves. I also pledged to work with each of the flowers in the relevant mansions of the labyrinth so that energy would flow upwards from my Sun pyramid to heal my heart.

"Remember that each circuit of the labyrinth heals mind, body and spirit, and that there are seven possible levels of healing in the labyrinth," reminded the Lion. "Or, to put it another way, when you've completed all Sacred Seven turns for the first time, then you can always begin again at a higher level of vibration, i.e. greater spiritual awareness."

"And furthermore, in that respect, there are actually three spiritual levels of Sun. For there is your own solar system Sun, your galactic central Sun and the Central Sun of all Central Suns; this latter is the Sacred Heart of the Creator from which All flows woven with

Love out of Light. At the moment you can work with the first Sun level, healing and growing spiritually. Then, if you choose to continue your journey on the Way of Love and Light, I can gradually guide you towards channelling the higher vibrations of Sun energy."

There was suddenly a startling burst of brilliant violet and golden light.

"Exactly!" said the Phoenix, who had materialised within the apex of the pyramid. "The trick is to understand that on this quest transformational new beginnings are always possible, each at a higher level of vibration and spiritual consciousness than the last." Just as instantly he vanished again, but something within me, the Sun sphere and pyramid of my own whose rays had started to flow upwards to awaken my heart and that resonated with this glorious Sun Bird, told me that he would soon return.

The Lion stood once again at my side, and I held out my hand towards him. Instantly the energy flowed, but this time I was amazed to sense that it flowed the other way, from my palm into the Lion. "You see," he smiled, "with the power of the Sun within you are already able to channel some healing energy." In this optimistic mood the Lion escorted me out of the mansion and left along the glittering crystal corridor still bright with sunshine.

Eventually this corridor came to an end and we turned to the left. Here another corridor started going the opposite way. As we made the right-angle turn I felt a consciousness-shift within my brain, but as I reflected on this, the Lion announced: "Here I leave you, but I have two gifts that you will need during a certain part of the quest. The first is a miniature Sun, reminding you of the power you now have within, and the second is a star tetrahedron of which Raphael spoke, symbol of all four elements and of yourself healed and balanced." So saying, he placed these on the ground. As I thanked him and put them both in my rucksack, he returned from whence he had come, leaving me secure in the knowledge that my mind, body and spirit healing and my masculine/feminine balance had truly begun.

Chapter 2

Mansion of Uranus & Fire

🕊 *Transformation through fires of passion and alchemy*

Thoughtfully I continued down this new corridor that curved gently to the left. The roof was made of warm coloured crystal that looked like topaz and the reddish granite floor sparkled with mica chips. As the bright sun shone through the corridor, it was lit with deep golden rays, as soft and honey-coloured as those of a languorous summer evening as the sun sinks westwards. In due course, as with the previous corridor, I suddenly came upon a large niche, this time to my right, that contained a curious curved gate. It had an oval-shaped top and was set snugly into the wall. The gate was sandalwood, carved with patterns set with stones of orange carnelian, citrine and topaz that winked in the light from the crystal corridor. I could also see flowers and symbols of fire and alchemy that I recognised. In front of the gate was a large Dragon, although like the Lion he, too, was benign-looking rather than frightening. He had a golden body, but silver wings and tail. I noticed that the end of his tail was set with three crystalline feathers. "I am pleased to see that you have made it." he breathed. "To pass this gate you need to answer some questions. Firstly tell me the name of the Angel Ruler of Fire whose mansion this is. "That's easy", I replied.

"You also need to name my specific title, and finally to name the flower and one of the alchemical Fire symbols on the gate," added the Dragon somewhat sternly. "Excellent!" beamed the Dragon, as I replied. "You may pass." At his words, the gate opened to reveal a most interesting chamber. It was huge and sort of spherical, with an oval domed roof, and it glowed with a mottled, yellowish-gold light. I soon saw that the reason for this was that it was made entirely from translucent amber blocks, some of which contained leafy inclusions. As the sun shone through the amber it cast strange and mysterious shadows. The floor, too, was curved to a level far below the one on which the gate was placed. The effect was like standing on the threshold of a giant hollow egg. A tripod arrangement, actually three lots of steps, led upwards from where I stood to an amber platform containing a triangular white bed, in the very heart of the egg-shaped sphere. It looked like a crucible, as pure blue-white fire flickered

and danced up the steps and around the platform, casting more fascinating reflections onto the floor of the chamber – it was all beautiful but rather daunting. As I paused, the Dragon entered and, before I could change my mind, I followed him.

The egg, a symbol of rebirth, I mused, wondering what to do next. There was a pale gold and blue-white lightning flash, and a dazzling presence was suddenly there in front of me – the Ruler of Fire and Alchemy himself.

"Welcome, daughter of man," proclaimed the angel. "What is it that you wish to do?"

"I want to change my life for the better, to find inner peace," I replied. "Then you have come to the right place," announced the angel. "This is the Chamber of Uranus and Transformation, wrought with amber – the fire of a thousand suns. It is for mind, body and spirit healing – primarily for the second of your energy centres, the one of transformation, innovation and creativity. Can you state which one this is?" I answered, and he exclaimed "That is right. Here is a real chance for brand new beginnings. I can help you start to make change really happen, but first you must find a way to reach the platform, for that is your crucible for the Fire alchemy."

Immediately I knew what to do. "Phoenix, Phoenix, Phoenix," I called. "Please tell me how to reach the platform, if it is for my highest good." The centre of the domed amber roof opened, like petals on a giant tiger-lily flower, and the Phoenix swooped down.

"This particular blue-white Fire of Alchemy has been known for thousands of years as Fire of Life," he informed me, "and it will not harm you, for it is also called the Flame That Does Not Burn. Just focus your entire will and intent on that fact for a moment or two, filling your heart with this knowledge, and then when you are ready you must walk fearlessly up the steps." I did as he suggested. Sure enough, he was right, and to the delight of the watching beings I ascended the steps unharmed to the central amber platform. There I lay down on the blue-white crucible that was as pure as the ashes from which the Phoenix dies and arises re-born. The angel took a small white fireball out of the Fire of Life. At its heart was a glowing white ember. "The first focus is mind and fear of change, as this can affect all your energy centres, not just the sacral one," he commented, and continued, "so with your permission, first I am going to transform away some of this fear." As he passed the ember right down my body, I felt an immediate sense of mental release, relating to anxieties in my life that had indeed affected many of my chakras.

"Now, will in the blue-white flames themselves," he suggested. "Ask them to empower your mind, to help you to release old programming in your sacral chakra that blocks the energy from rising through the meridian from lower self to heart." I followed his instructions and the blue-white flames flickered around the lower half of my body; the essence of them passed within. As I looked within I saw that the pyramid that had started forming within me was now more distinct and Fire energy was rising through its apex and flowing upwards towards my heart. "You see," he commented, "now you have done two-thirds of the work to empower your energy flow upwards; when you've worked in the Mars Mansion you will have fully formed your Fire pyramid to free the blocks to your heart space. Next, Nathaniel will offer normal Fire healing to help you replenish the specific orange chakra of your body a little more. Finally, I shall return to assist you with spiritual harmony."

The white flames vanished and pure orange flames appeared in their place, encircling the crucible. These flames then formed the shape of another angel with fiery orange Light wings. "I am Nathaniel," pronounced this being. "If you can describe my Guardianship then you will benefit greatly." As I answered correctly, Nathaniel pointed his right hand towards my sacral chakra centre and caused orange rays to flow directly towards it. "This is healing essence of Fire itself," he told me. It seemed to pass into my body and surround the flower in that energy centre and dark or cloudy areas were transmuted. I felt creativity stir within me, and the true desire for change and transformation strengthen.

"Whatever you wish to change or transform," advised Nathaniel, "you need to be fired with enthusiasm to carry it through. As you are in the Mansion of Uranus, ask to be filled with the Fire of passion," he went on. "It is for you to decide what you need passion for; it could be for sexuality, for life itself, for a cause, for a brand new start or all of these – whatever is right for you – and it is for you to truly will and intend your transformation to begin." Mentally I asked for my new beginnings to be filled with passion for all of these, and

I saw the orange flower within me had lost its translucence and become very distinct. "Even though the focus here is mainly on the orange energy centre, you can learn to use this Fire to empower your whole body," added Nathaniel. "It just takes knowledge of the power of your will combined with trust and belief. We will help you to work at that. Now it is time for some spiritual harmony."

With that, the Ruler of Fire reappeared, holding a kind of giant tuning fork. I regarded the tuning fork with interest. "What note does that emit?" I asked. "Why, any note you need," he replied. "It also works at many levels. In this mansion the Cosmic Tuning Fork will firstly place this, your orange chakra centre, in harmony with Mother Earth, and the other planets of your Solar System, as all are linked. You will be able to see your orange flower become ever clearer and brighter as it heals further. But you need to ask that whatever happens is for your highest good. Also, this doesn't mean that you need no more healing, as it will not, of itself, clear all deep-seated blocks – these require some further work by you – but it will give you a strong start."

As he struck the tuning fork and placed it against the amber couch on which I lay, the cosmic vibration started. I willed it firstly to aid physical and spiritual harmony in my orange energy centre. The vibration in fact ran through my body, starting at my toes and exiting through my crown, leaving me especially tingling in the region of that centre. I looked inwards from my heart and I saw that the glowing orange flower was now radiating this colour out to my aura.

"Can it work for the other energy centres?" I asked.

"Yes, all mansions will have a general as well as a specific healing effect," he replied. "The healing vibration subtly changes for each energy centre, for the lower ones are a denser vibration than the higher ones. See!" he smiled, and as he struck it again a magical thing happened, for the sound vibration changed as it rippled over me from head to toe and then back again to head, and once more to toe. As the energy surged through my feet to harmonise with Earth and out through my crown to the Solar System it felt absolutely wonderful, as if my body itself could sing for the joy in life. Only then did I begin to realise how tired and low I had felt before starting this quest and that this feeling had become my norm. I thanked the angel with all my heart. "However, there are no real short cuts. It will be even more effective when you have worked on all of your energy centres in turn," he counselled. "There are also different levels of vibration depending on which one you are ready for at any one time," he continued, rather cryptically.

"I don't understand," I said. "Well it's rather like the Solar Lion and the three levels of Suns," he replied. "As I advised, you do need to be willing to commit to self-healing and therefore to doing some work on each energy centre. Wherever you start the process, they all need some attention. But if you do this, the Cosmic Tuning Fork's first level of healing vibrations, apart from balancing all chakras, as we've said, aids you to be in physical and spiritual harmony with Mother Earth and your Solar System vibration. Then, if you continue with your pledge to self-heal and develop spiritual consciousness, at an appropriate time the tuning fork's vibration will rise, helping you next to become harmonised with your Milky Way galaxy. Finally, if you really pledge to aid the cause of Love and Light, the tuning fork will assist you towards becoming harmonised with the Universe and All, for this is the true objective of travelling along the Way of Love and Light. And then to go back and show others the Way further enhances the Divine connection with All."

"Now you have started healing both yellow and orange chakra centres, look within and see what has happened to your Sun/Fire pyramid." I looked, and I saw that energy was now flowing strongly upwards towards my heart. "Now it is time to move on," advised the Ruler of Fire, "for you are ready for the next challenge, that is the Mansion of Mars and Earth."

I climbed down from the couch, and descended the steps, back through the sandalwood door. "Don't forget that you've only just completed the start of the very first level of labyrinthine healing," reminded the Dragon, "and when you are ready, come back and see us again – you still have so much to learn."

I turned my attention to the Dragon, and immediately, a question struck me. "What is the significance of your gold and silver body?" I asked him. "I know what the Caduceus looks like, as there are two snakes around the staff, one gold and one silver, and they meet at the wings (brow chakra). But you seem to have both together in one body. And can you also tell me: what do the three crystal feathers on the end of your tail signify?" I added. "Well there is a whole lesson for you in this. I hold both gold and silver vibrations in harmony," smiled the Dragon, "for I epitomise perfect mind/body balance of masculine and feminine energies which terminate at the third eye. And so I am spiritually unified, creating the Trinity, or, to put it another way, I am the embodiment of Unity Consciousness that manifests at Crown chakra level. This means that in terms of spiritual awareness I represent Oneness with All. This is what you are ultimately searching for, as it is a state of Bliss where you will achieve total inner peace."

"The three feathers symbolise both the Trinity and Hermes Trismegistos' Law of Three that underpins All. For example, you humans measure time in three, your bodies are based on carbon, oxygen and hydrogen and so forth. Also, the three feathers represent the three levels of unity with Mother Earth, then with the Galaxy, and finally with the Universe. They are also for the three suns: your own solar Sun, the Galactic Central Sun and the Central Sun of all Suns who is also named Mazuriel, the Sacred Heart of the Creator. And many of your belief systems hold Trinities, from Ancient Egypt, Isis, Osiris, Horus to that of Christian and other faiths."

"Finally, because my three feathers are hollow crystal they hold the healing energies of ultimate Truth: gold, silver and sapphire, carried through the diamond ray of Cosmic Spirit, or Creation. Eventually you may reach this point yourself, as you move towards enlightenment with the help of the angels. Then you can channel Cosmic Spirit yourself to help heal Mother Earth and all sentient life. By the way, I have a gift for you," and so saying, he gave me a small amber egg. I thanked him and placed it in my rucksack, mulling over his rather puzzling answer as I continued to walk to the end of the topaz corridor. I turned the next right angle, and once again I experienced that definite consciousness shift; everything he had said made sense. At any rate, if not yet in my mind, it made perfect sense in my heart. I also knew that my own transformation was well under way.

Chapter 3

Mansion of Mars & Earth
🖋 *Courage and forgiveness allow security and empowerment*

The curved corridor that I now stood in had a floor of terracotta laid in an attractive herringbone pattern, and the roof was of thin panels of red agate striped with translucent white. The sun, low on the horizon, shone through this roof reflecting both light and shade, conferring warmth and comfort. After quite a long time, I came to a niche on my left that by now I knew would be the gateway to the next mansion. Indeed, in front of me was an archway of lustrous polished red marble veined in deep purple, within which stood a pair of mahogany gates bound with wrought iron. Within these were carved flowers, symbolic of the energy centre to be addressed here, and embellished with beautiful glowing red gems that I took to be rubies and garnets. Iron sconces held torches to provide more light. But more amazing than all this was the magnificent She-Leopard who lay in front of the gates; she regarded me calmly with her emerald eyes. "You need to answer three questions to go further," she informed me. "Tell me which angel is associated with this mansion to aid you with courage, and the metal that links with this being."

As I answered this for her she nodded her great head and then she asked: "With which energy centre of your body is this angel associated?" Again I answered her. "Finally, what extra qualities do I offer you, that combine with those of the Angel Ruler?" On hearing my answer she commented, "Note that well, my child," then gracefully rose to her feet and stood to one side. As she did so the gates opened and I saw that inside was a being with a blue gaze and huge crimson and magenta Light wings. I knew it to be the Ruler of Mars himself.

"This is the Mansion of Mars and it links with Earth," he announced, "because mankind has had connections with that planet for hundreds of thousands of years." He motioned me to enter. The chamber was square and spacious and its roof was translucent coral that allowed a warm light to penetrate from above, like the summer sun called the Blood Rose, rising through mist as it dawns over the horizon. Illumination also came from bright flames leaping from within an iron bowl. The bowl was mounted on a square-topped wrought-iron

stand, with red marble steps leading up to it. At first I thought that my eyes deceived me, for the strange thing about the flames was that they glowed in different colours – now crimson, now scarlet, now a sort of burgundy or purple-red. Now and again there were touches of vivid magenta as the colours coalesced and flashed diamond sparkles of light. They must be mind, body and spirit colours, I thought to myself.

"You surmise that these flames represent mind, body and spirit, and you are not wrong," commented the Ruler of Mars, reading my mind. "The basic crimson is my colour for courage as well as for empowerment, while when it becomes bright ruby with crystal sparkles it is the shade of energy and wellbeing of the angel Mumiah. The purple-red is for security, strong foundations in life, a shade by the way that links also with Earth and my fellow angel Ariel. All these aid mainly mind and body. As for the magenta, this represents pure spirit, and it is for when you involve your heart and soul in all matters. Then the colours of pink and blue are added to the red, producing magenta," he explained.

"My Leopard aids you to work on this although you will only understand the true meaning of magenta if you complete the quest," he added. "Which do you feel you need?" he asked. "Once again, I need them all," I replied immediately.

At these words, there was a swirl of diamond energy, shot through with scarlet and ruby red, and Mumiah appeared. "Let's start with aspects of mind involving bodily energy and wellbeing," she suggested. "Now take your consciousness within and visualise the flower you have seen in that part of your body." As I did so, she said: "Now step up to the bowl of fire and focus all your will and intent – now very strong and powerful after your work with yellow – on breathing in the essence of the scarlet sparkling flames. I am here to help you really absorb this energy, taking it right down to the correct energy centre. See it surround and empower the red flower within you so that it bursts into life and light." I followed her instructions and, standing in front of the bowl of flames, I asked to breathe in their powerful energy and draw it right down through my body. Sure enough, as the flower became more distinct and opened to its full ruby splendour I, too, began to feel stronger, filled with vitality, the blood coursing round my body.

"Now you can breathe this healing energy into the other chakra centres," suggested Mumiah. I closed my eyes and focused on continuing to breathe in the sparkling wellbeing flames, all the time sensing their ability to bring vigour. As I breathed out, I let go of tiredness, inertia, lack of stamina and inability to see things through to the end, until I felt that my actual blood contained these sparkles and flowed more vigorously around my body. As I was savouring this feeling, a third angel appeared, emitting Light rays of pale amethyst threaded with slate grey, purple and lavender blue. He appeared to balance the earth below him and the sky above him, and I knew it was Ariel, ruler of the elements of Earth and Air.

"Now we need to ground you properly," he advised. "Approach the bowl and breathe in purple-red. Send the energy down to your red flower, deepening the shade a little, and then through your legs, into your feet and from your feet into the ground below. Imagine you are sending it to heal Mother Earth herself." As I followed his instructions, I felt myself grounded and balanced, and as I sent this crimson-purple light to Mother Earth, I felt her responding by sending me sapphire-blue energy in return. This gift of energy from the Mother I absorbed into all my energy centres and therefore all the other flowers. Once again, the orange and yellow flowers glowed even more brightly while the rest improved a bit. "I know," I said, "there's still work to do on many of them, but I am getting there." At these words the ruby flower seemed to glow brilliantly. "You see," smiled Ariel, "your resolve is adding to the fact that you are now creating firm foundations within the root of yourself, upon which you will build in future. For there is very little chance of you completing your life transformation without grounding and securing your foundations. And your desire to help Mother Earth also works in your favour."

"Now to consider your core values in this energy centre – let's talk about my attributes of courage, justice and empowerment," invited the Ruler of Mars. "For you have a major block there and you need to look at the cause," he informed me. "To give a hint, my Snow Leopard has given you good advice already."

"I am not very good at guessing games," I murmured as I reflected on his words, although deep down I knew very well what he was talking about because it concerned my parents. I

was the oldest of three daughters, and we all felt our father would have liked sons rather than daughters. Also, it's true to say that I have always believed that no matter how hard I tried at everything, my father didn't think I was good enough and whatever I did he always praised my sisters more; he did the same to them as well. Perhaps it was some kind of strategy he had, to make us all work as hard as possible, but actually it only made for unhappiness.

The other great problem I had had was electing to work for him in the family business. Starting at the bottom, I wanted to obtain early promotion, but no matter how much effort I put in I didn't seem to get very far. My father bent over backward so hard not to favour me that I felt he actually discriminated against me, in terms of financial reward and promotion. In the end I had to emigrate to prove to myself that I was capable enough to get on in an organisation. Then, when I returned two years later, after a disastrous love affair, I made the mistake of going back into the family firm, thinking that now I'd proved my capability I would be made a manager. I succeeded in obtaining a title and thought that I'd finally made my mark. But the glow didn't last, as one of the other managers didn't accept my authority over her, and when I laid down ground rules she just went over my head to my father.

"And your father didn't back you up," observed Camael, who of course knew everything there was to know, past, present and future. "No he didn't," I replied, "he backed her instead and so completely undermined my position. Eventually, after about fifteen years of this I left and went to work for another organisation, and that was the first time I felt actually valued as being intelligent, a good organiser and efficient in interpersonal skills.

The other issue was that when I was young, I felt I was rather a plain child and not pretty enough for my beautiful mother. She had been a beauty queen in her teens, and I thought I was something of a disappointment to her in that respect. This may have been wrong, as she was basically an unhappy woman due to my father's 'straying' ways, but it left me always feeling I had to strive harder and harder to try to win their approval. Whilst I am sure they loved me, and my childhood was fine in other ways, these uncertainties had a devastating effect on my self-confidence for many years. In fact, I had always lacked self-confidence, both in my work and in myself. "I suppose you mean I still need to resolve this issue?" I ventured.

"Indeed, as even though both parents have died, the forgiveness issue, coupled with that lack of confidence it has caused through your life so far, is holding you back from the ability to feel secure and to open your higher heart, a key part of your spiritual progress. Now you and I can bring forward the essence of these persons into this room. What you need is to determine mentally that you can now display the courage, tenderness and greatness of heart to show complete forgiveness. Even though you were not at fault yourself, there are probably also issues that in retrospect you are sorry about." I agreed that perhaps I had been unsympathetic to my mother's unhappiness, and too busy trying to prove myself better than my father in his own business, which must have been difficult for them both. All these thoughts I had kept inside me for years.

Then said the Ruler of Mars: "Will and intend that you can bring the power of your base chakra up to the heart, to combine these two energies. Finally, if you go to the bowl of flames and breathe in the magenta fire, it will actually strengthen and empower you to do what needs to be done in this chamber, for it's not quite enough to forgive them – should you not ask their blessing also and forgive yourself?"

Once more I regarded the bowl of flames. I applied the whole of my willpower to do as he suggested, focusing on the potential power of the fully opened heart, and then I breathed deeply of the magenta fire. Then, on the other side of the plinth and bowl, I perceived two transparent shapes materialising – my father and mother. Immediately, tears came to my eyes, for both had died very suddenly without giving me any opportunity to say goodbye or to resolve past issues. I wept for my loss, for though it was true that I had nursed certain resentments, I had loved them both very much.

No matter how justified my resentment was, I could see that Camael was right. This issue was undoubtedly blocking my spiritual progress in this life. I faced the ghostly figures and looked them both in the eye. "With all my heart I forgive you and I am truly sorry for any way that I upset you or was not a dutiful daughter," I announced. The spirit of my mother came forward and embraced me, by which I mean that she seemed to flow around me before de-materialising. Then the spirit of my father smiled and held out his hand, offering me a small, square sandalwood box. The box was solid even though the hand was ghostly. I took the box, whereupon the figure bowed, faded and disappeared.

I regarded the box, but it seemed to be solid – I could not see how to open it. I shook it and it rattled, so it definitely contained something. "When the time comes the box will open," advised the Ruler of Mars. "At this point you only need to know that it contains the true potential of your higher heart," he went on. "You have made a good start on freeing up your root chakra to be strong and secure, and this will commence your personal empowerment. You may even feel physically stronger down in your lower self as you've also added the red flames to the Sun, Earth and Fire pyramid you now carry there and so completed it. The clarified red, orange and yellow energies can combine to heal your IBS, as well as flowing upwards towards your heart. The healing of your heart will move on much more in the next mansion."

"At the right moment, your loving will and intent will release the contents of this gift. These you will keep until the Wisdom Mansion. It's to do with the real power of magenta, which resembles Hermes Trismegistos' triple crown of Love, Power and Wisdom, inasmuch as this shade defines the wisdom that comes from using the power of unconditional and non-judgemental Love." I thought deeply about this and about using heart to fully empower all other energy centres. "Now you can exit this mansion and continue the quest." And so saying, he disappeared, leaving a ruby glow behind him.

I found I was once again standing by the mahogany gates. They slowly opened to let me back through to where the She-Leopard still reclined in all her stately splendour. She rose to her feet and stood before me in the corridor of red-and-white agate. "You have done exceptionally well, and so I will lead you to the next mansion," she offered, as she started to pad along the corridor. This curved gently to the right, and as I hurried along to keep up she said: "Just remember that although you have made an excellent start, in time you will reach another level; then you may feel you need to return and do more remedial work on the red, orange and yellow energy centres of lower self. If so, I shall look forward to seeing you again." That said, as the corridor came to an end she vanished.

Chapter 4

Mansion of Moon, Neptune & Water
Moon gifts Hope and water brings Tranquillity

I turned a right-angled corner to the right and once again I felt that shift within my brain as my spiritual consciousness took a kind of leap. It seemed to me that this was because my energies were now focusing more in my heart, and it was enough to power me along a strange new corridor. The roof was of clear green calcite, while the floor was of translucent green crystal that looked like nephrite jade. The sun shone through this crystalline roof, giving a cool and gentle diffused radiance, so that it seemed as if I was walking through watery depths; I almost expected to see fish swimming towards me. I didn't see any as such, but then I formed the impression that I was in a crystal corridor filled with air but that somehow the ocean was certainly below me. It grew dimmer and I realised that the sun was waning rapidly. The corridor curved gradually to the left and in due course I came upon a niche set into the wall on my right. Within this niche was a Water Gate carved from elm and embossed with patterns of shining silver full and crescent moons and other symbols outlined in pearls, embellished with emeralds and aquamarine – water of the sea. In front of it was a semi-circular pool that obviously extended on the other side as well. Half-in, half-out of the pool was a magnificent Dolphin. So it really is water below where I am standing, I thought to myself.

"Greetings," said the Dolphin, "and welcome to the Mansion of Moon and Neptune, and the healing power of Water. Congratulations! You have passed through the three mansions of lower self and you have reached this, the fourth, which is the first of the two heart chambers. Here you will address healing the personal heart to enable you to cross what we call the heart bridge, leading to the three mansions connected with higher self. After those, the final step is the Place of the Higher Heart. If you succeed in reaching the end of this quest," he added, for good measure and encouragement.

"First of all, though, you need to enter this mansion. To pass through the Water Gate you must be prepared to enter the ocean itself, which is beneath the mansion. Also you must

answer several questions. Firstly, tell me two names: the name of the Angel who is Ruler of Neptune and Lord of the Waters of Earth and Powers of the Moon (in terms of the tides). Also the name of the Angel Ruler of the Moon herself." As I gave the right answers to the Dolphin, he then asked, "Now tell me a crystal associated with the moon, and then which crystal's actual name means water of the sea." As I again answered correctly he nodded his great head and motioned me to enter the half-moon shaped pool. "You need to swim under the Water Gate, but you will have no problem as these pools are very deep," he advised.

"But I am afraid of deep water," I replied. "There is no need for any fear within the Sacred Space of this labyrinth," he admonished firmly, "for you can come to no harm whatsoever in the care of the angels. Indeed it is fear that constricts the soul while love expands it and you learned this in the Mansion of Mars and Earth. See, I am here to take you through," and he offered me his flipper. As I entered the pool, holding onto the flipper, I focused upon my red flower for more courage and as I did so, a marvellous thing happened. I felt a vibration from the Dolphin that came through his flipper into my hand, then travelled like a wave through my heart, dissolving my fear completely. As it exited from my body it took with it the negative energy that had been my fear of being out of my depth. "Why, that's amazing!" I cried. "It's the healing power of Water and its effect will last," promised the Dolphin, "if you believe it will."

"What do you want to do here?" the Dolphin then asked. "I should like to continue my self-forgiveness, and heal my personal heart of past hurts, so that I can combine it with all my other energy centres and work towards opening my higher heart," I replied. "It is good that you have determined that," replied the Dolphin, "as this wisdom is the step you needed to access the healing power of Water more fully. The power involves spheres and pyramids again. Firstly it's a circular process, which is why the central island is circular. Moon energy can activate the forming of a Moon sphere within you over the heart chakras (like Sun energy and the Sun sphere you now hold over solar and sacral chakras)."

"But also the Moon rules the tides of Earth and the flow of certain liquids within you. Moon, Air and Water healing is symbolised by a downward-pointing pyramid as opposed to the Sun, Earth and Fire upward-pointing pyramid" the Dolphin continued. This means that when you integrate both energy pyramids (they would look like the star crystal that the Solar Lion gave you), you have accessed all the powers of the four elements within you, and they help complete a level of self-healing. As the Ruler of the Sun informed you, whatever gender you are born in, all humans have both masculine and feminine aspects to heal and balance". As I tried to take this in he went on "In time you will understand fully, now let's proceed as there's lots to do here!"

Without more ado we swam under the Water Gate and as I climbed out of the water I saw the Moon had risen (it looked much larger than usual). I found myself within a vast chamber in the shape of an icosahedron (which I knew to be the Platonic solid for water). Suspended within this was a huge downward-pointing crystal pyramid, reached by a crystal bridge extending through a gap in one side. As I stood upon the bridge the pyramid's four walls extended up, out and away from me and the central point was way below. It was like the Sun Mansion's pyramid but inverted and with a circular space in the square top that was open to the moonlit night. I was beginning to realise that the Sacred Seven Mansions were not exactly part of the labyrinth, but merely accessed from it. Just below the level at which I was standing (about half-way up the pyramid's side) it was filled with clear water that rippled like silk. I felt as if I was standing on a crystal diving board waiting to enter that beautiful water. In the centre floated a shining spherical shape, while spaced around it were six huge emerald water-lily leaves. As I looked down it gave the effect of looking at a giant six-petal flower shape with a silvery white heart.

The whole space was lit with bright Moon rays that sparkled and played on the water and lily leaves, and as this light fell on the spherical island I saw that it was made from selenite. For the sphere captured the moonbeam in a shining silver-white line that shimmered straight towards me across the water beneath my feet. I now saw that above this miniature Moon floated the two Light beings who jointly ruled the Mansion. One radiated pure silvery white luminescence and had palest turquoise Light wings, while from the second presence deeper aqua rays of turquoise and emerald swirled and flowed around like water itself. If you truly

desire to cleanse and heal your heart," spoke the first (from whom a scent of lilies wafted), "you may come to this Sacred Healing Space."

"Oh I do," I swiftly replied, and the Dolphin looked pleased. "Well, now you must swim here along that moonlight path," said the Lord of the Waters and Powers of the Moon. After my earlier discussion with the Dolphin, I now felt able to dive into the water without fear, and swim to the floating island. As I drew closer I saw that it was really a curved hollow bowl open at one side and in the centre of the top, and as the angels caused it to remain steady, I pulled myself up and went inside it, as the Dolphin clicked his approval. The crystal was translucent so that the moonbeams cast a gentle radiance within.

"We are delighted that you have come," the angels told me, motioning me to lie down on a green bed, whereupon, as I obeyed, they glided to either side of me. I lay down and looked directly upwards; above me was a round hole that allowed me to see the corresponding hole in the crystal pyramid's square roof way above me. Immediately above this a full Moon shone through all. "Now you are resting on water, balanced between the silver sphere in the heavens and its counterpart here below," announced Gabrielle. "We are going to address mind first, but what is important is to link this with heart, for that is the way towards true balance. What are the issues you need to heal?"

"Well, I still lack self-belief. On a personal front, for a long time my lack of self-confidence affected my ability to make lasting relationships with men," I replied. "As a teenager I was painfully shy and felt I didn't have much to offer. Probably this showed when I went out with friends, as I did not enjoy great success at dances. It was the early days of rock and roll; I couldn't jive, had a dread of being invited to dance, and was often a bit of a wallflower. It is said that other people take you at your own face value, and perhaps that is why I did not find a boyfriend until I was around eighteen years old. In time I did overcome the shyness, but I was what used to be called a late developer, and it was not until my mid-twenties that I started to form any kind of view of the kind of man I'd like to settle down with. Before that I chose the wrong men entirely and had one disastrous love affair. Then when I was twenty-five I met the right man, and have been happily married ever since."

"Indeed you found your twin-flame, as he needed to support your Light Work in this life path," commented the Lord of the Waters. "In past lives you supported him, now it's his turn, but almost everyone has a damaged heart, sometimes from past lifetimes, including you. Is there anything else you can tell me?"

"I now see that in business terms the same lack of confidence applied. In fact before he died I was still desperately trying to prove to my father that I was more capable than he seemed to think, and successful in my field, and I think that the stress of that caused my IBS. I drove myself too hard." "You are correct in that surmise," asserted Gabrielle. "To help you finally deal with this and learn to accept yourself, faults and all, we are going to create a spiral of moonbeams (in fact this is the Moon counterpart of what you did in the Sun Mansion). You see, as Dolphin told you, to really heal yourself you need to achieve both Moon and Sun, masculine and feminine balances within you," continued the Ruler of the Moon. "But most of all you need to love yourself."

She continued: "Breathe in deeply, focus on your heart and will and intend that the essence of my silver Moon energy spiral flows into you. See a sphere of silver forming within you, overlapping the golden Sun one, and know that it holds power of cleansing and purifying your personal heart and greatly expanding your intuition." Indeed it was true, for as I breathed in the Moon rays through the aperture in the roof, a silver spiral of Moon energy poured down and like a gentle silver fountain it flowed into my heart space to form a balancing moon sphere within me. I could feel its radiance extending all around into the other energy centres.

"Now for the healing power of Water of Life itself," stated the Lord of the Waters, "for this also boosts the powers of the Moon as well as harnessing those of Neptune." For this we create a triangular funnel woven out of moonbeams, echoing the shape of this pyramid. As this amazing Light funnel appeared, through it flowed a sparkling stream of Water of Life directly into my heart space, washing away the hurts and damage. And when I looked within I could perceive that the water-lily pad and bud had become bright and solid, cradled within my own internal Moon sphere. Then I saw that that it had also created a Moon/Water pyramid within me, balancing the Sun, Earth and Fire one, its power radiating out to heal and balance me.

"In the Mercury Mansion you will add Air to complete this pyramid, but meanwhile will and intend that this power of Moon within continues to aid you to heal your heart and love yourself unconditionally. For this is the preliminary process of opening your higher heart flower," suggested the Lord of the Waters. As I did so, I felt that lack of confidence and insecurity from past relationships float away. As I released these, I could sense the emerald leaf and bud intensify in colour; a tiny bit of the magenta flower was visible, as a wonderful sense of calmness and tranquillity filled my heart and spread through me.

"If you so choose, with loving intent, you can now give thanks by returning healing to the Water of Life in this mansion, for it is a microcosm of any and all of the waters of Earth," suggested the angels. "Earth is a water planet and mankind is more than seventy percent water." And so I did. I sent Love and Light to the waters around me in the chamber. Then Water of Life sprayed back to me from the centre of the water-lily leaves in six beautiful, symmetrical fountains, to the delight of the Dolphin. "Keep healing it!" he cried. "The more you send out healing, the more you will receive it back, and it is this that opens your higher heart," he told me. "And furthermore, the desire to help All is the way to complete the Quest of the Heart."

Finally, as I swam back to the Water Gate, he picked up something in his great beak and offered it to me. I saw that it was a large silvery blue-green pearl. "This is a symbol of your own hidden potential," he told me. "It's a pearl of great price, as is your own talent, and it is time for you to bring this forth to help others. You have much to do in this connection." I regarded this beautiful pearl, wondering how I could possibly have something this wonderful hidden metaphorically within my heart and soul. Humbly I accepted his precious gift, thanked him and placed it very carefully in my rucksack.

Chapter 5

Magical Mansion of Pluto

Angelic Light Magic illumines your heart

In this calm and tranquil mood, and with a peaceful heart, I let the Dolphin escort me back under the Water Gate. As I swam under it with him, holding his flipper, it seemed that energy was flowing from my own palm back to the Dolphin. This time the energy was cool. "Yes, you are giving me healing energy," he confirmed, "for in sending healing to the waters of Earth you have been granted the ability to channel healing power of Water whenever you wish. Goodbye for now!" he cried as he disappeared back into the pool.

Although I had spent many hours in the Mansion of Moon, Neptune & Water it was still night above me. The moon still shone through the green crystal roof and I was alone, but I did not have far to travel. The corridor curved left for a while and then came to an abrupt halt. I realised I must be close to the centre of the labyrinth. There was a right-angle turn to the left and again my spiritual consciousness shifted up a notch, allowing me to begin to process my recent amazing experiences. I started to walk down a new, lighter corridor curving to the right, whose roof was of clear pink and lavender lepidolite crystal. A strange, ethereal light filtered through this roof and, looking up, I saw that Moon, Sun and Stars were all in the sky simultaneously, shining radiantly down on me. That must be because I am now coming to the place where the veil between realities is thin, where Earth meets Air, I reflected.

After a while the expected niche appeared on my left, containing a mysterious gate with metal cross pieces and sacred geometry symbols, the whole thing surrounded by swirling mists of white, grey and violet. The top half of the gate was wreathed in pale mauve, lavender and white, while the lower half was deeper violet, purple and slate grey. In the very centre of the gate where the metal bars actually crossed there was a huge faceted amethyst crystal. As I stood regarding this gate with its beautiful crystal, the mists coalesced and seemed to form a shape – indeed it was Ariel who materialised.

"Welcome to my Magical Mansion," he proclaimed. "Of course you know me, but if you can name the attributes I bring you and the energy centre with which I am associated,

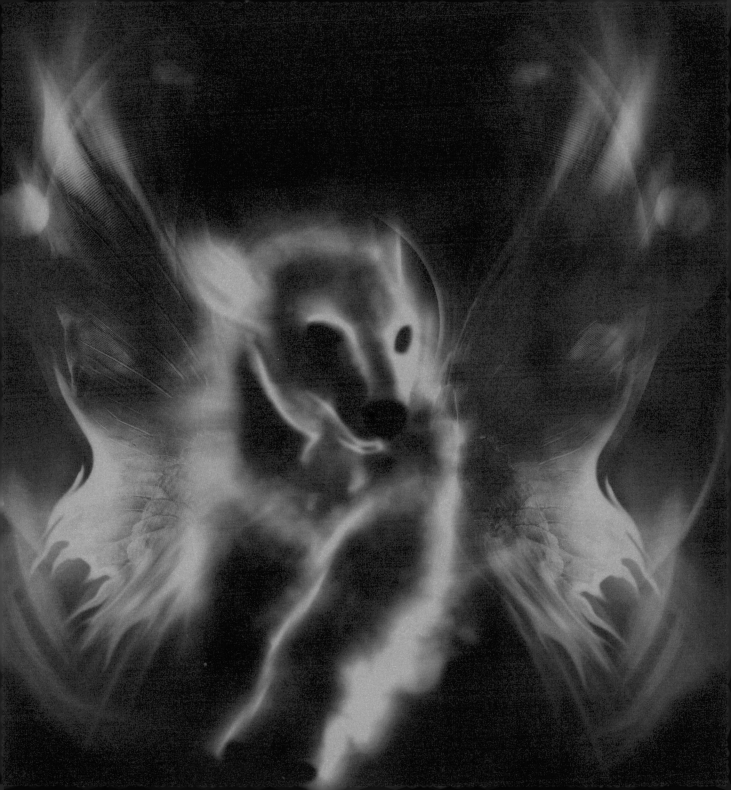

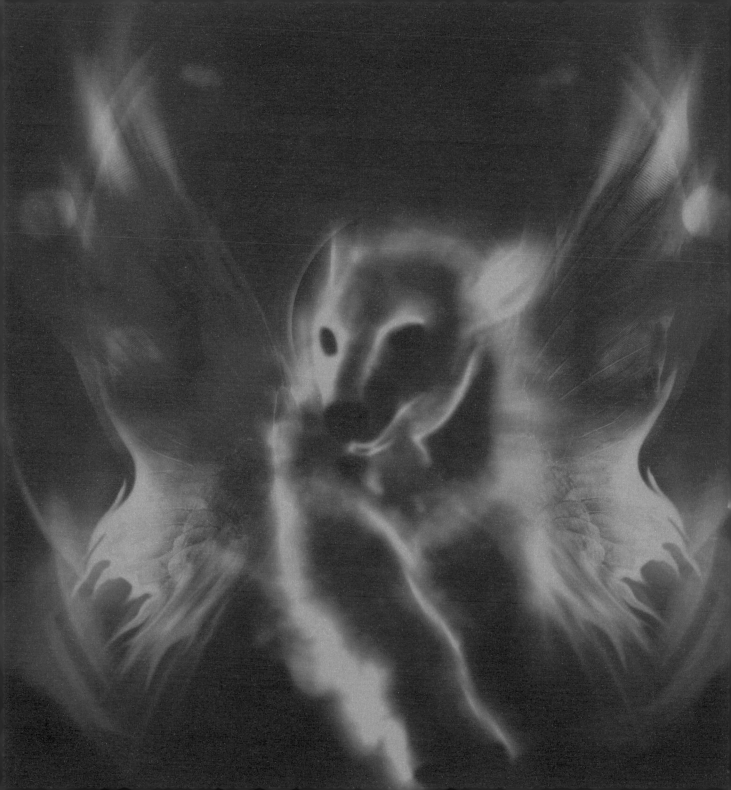

then I will tell you how to enter." I named these. Ariel smiled, as he did so the smoky violet, purple and mauve Light rays rippled around him, forming a Light cloak that also encompassed the gate. "Now, look closely at the amethyst crystal on this gate," he advised, "and tell me what you see." Approaching closer to the crystal, I looked into it. It seemed to contain the same Light that surrounded Ariel, but also twinkling within were pinpoints like tiny stars. "Why, it has stars in it!" I exclaimed. "Indeed that is so," replied Ariel. "But in truth it has more than that, as it is the Magical Mansion; it's inter-dimensional and in that sense it contains the whole of your Universe as well. "Do you want to go into this crystal?" "Yes, please," I said immediately, becoming used now to lightning decisions.

"All you have to do is use your heart and that willpower that you have learned," he instructed. "Just close your eyes, breathing deeply of this violet Light around me, and with your will and loving intent ask to enter the crystal for your highest good." I followed his instructions, closing my eyes, breathing deeply and slowly and asking with all the power of my will to go into this crystal. When I opened my eyes I found that I was indeed inside the faceted amethyst crystal. It was entirely filled with different shades of violet, cool blue, warm pink and silvery white-violet that glowed softly with the light of the stars scattered around its interior. As I looked it seemed that the whole mansion was expanding outwards at a rapid rate that made me giddy.

"Yes, it is indeed expanding, like your Universe itself." Ariel had read my mind, as well he might, being closely connected with that particular energy centre. Ariel then told me: "In accordance with the Law of Three, there are three different experiences for you in this mansion. Firstly, I am going to help you with some general body healing, using the power of amethyst itself, and because I assist Raphael with healing (particularly that connected with the element of Air – Breath of Life), this centres around your ability to breathe correctly. You see most of mankind does not even know how to breathe Breath of Life to the full, causing serious health issues around the element of Air. For instance, respiratory ailments, panic attacks, self-inflicted damage like smoking, and so forth, all involve Breath of Life. Many could be addressed by learning to breathe deeply and calmly rather than shallowly.

Correct breathing actually aids all energy centres to function properly. By the way, you have already considerably raised your level of vibration, and that means that you have strengthened your immune system. Viruses at a lower vibration than yours will be less able to attach to you now. Good news indeed."

Ariel indicated a kind of raised area formed of deep purple amethyst, inviting me to lie on it. As in the earlier mansions, it moulded itself to my body shape, as if it had been awaiting my arrival. He placed a mixture of clear and smoky quartz and amethyst crystals on my brow, upper chest, and lung areas. Then he caused Violet Fire of three different shades to flare up and around me, bathing me in this otherworldly radiance. At the same time he drew three flame shapes, each with a spiral around it, over those parts of me. He said: "The cool blue violet helps dispel heated emotions or pain within mind, the warm pink violet transmutes respiratory blocks, and the silvery violet promotes emotional intelligence and aids safe spiritual development of your psychic skills." As the three different Violet Fires flowed over and around me I felt washed clean within as well as in my aura.

"Thank you," I said at once. Of course I already knew that Violet Fire is the Light of Transmutation and also known as the spiritual antiseptic, but the three specific shades were new and useful information. Ariel went on: "You will now be able to channel as well as teach these different Violet Fire shades to aid self or others, and as part of this mansion's lesson I am also to instruct you how to use them as effectively as possible. As you are aware, violet is the Ray of Magic, always capable of rendering all dark negative energy back to Light, but mankind needs to know how to use all three shades."

"Please tell me more," I begged of Ariel. And he continued: "People can invoke my name and then say a mantra, such as 'I channel the power of Violet Fire that brings the purity I desire', three times. This would dispel negativity around them in a room, or it would surround them with protective violet Light. Similarly, they can say the mantra silently to transmute negativity within the mind. Or, they can imagine a bowl of Violet Fire and actually visualise throwing negative emotions, feelings, etc, into it to be transmuted back to pure white Light. All are very powerful!" I resolved to note down this information.

"Now for your remaining learning experiences in this mansion – do you want to travel to the Stars and beyond?" "I certainly do," I replied excitedly. "Well, now bring your eyes down to this mansion itself and look towards its exact centre." As I did so I saw a kind of amethyst dais, shaped like a flat six-pointed star. On it was a kind of chariot. Why, it's Rikbiel's Light Chariot of Love, though without his Twin Horses, I told myself. As I was wondering what this meant, a beautiful shimmering pastel rainbow of light appeared and once again Melchisadec, Ruler of Violet himself, was beside me in the chamber.

"You have a crystal connected with this mansion," commented Melchisadec. "I do," I agreed, and rummaged in the rucksack to retrieve it. "This is where you can use that crystal," suggested the angel. "For we now want to let you into a secret. Here you see Rikbiel's Light Vehicle in the familiar style of a Roman chariot, but in fact it is really a Merkaba Light Body. To travel safely to the Stars you need to be in a Merkaba, and with humans this is created through Love and the geometry of a star tetrahedron like the one you are holding. In fact it's an external representation of the crystal energy version you're creating inside yourself from combining the healing Pyramids of Sun, Earth and Fire, and Moon, Air and Water. It may surprise you to know that in due course you will be teaching people (with our help of course) how to form the Merkaba Light Body for themselves. Not only is it a healing tool, but also it's a key part of what some call Ascension. However, that's in the future. In the 'now' moment what you need to do is stand in the very centre of the platform, where the chariot is. Hold the crystal in both hands, and we will create the Merkaba around you. It is a saucer-shaped Light field that moves through space/time in right angles. This will raise your spiritual consciousness again as well as your third eye vibration, developing latent psychic skills."

I hastened to the platform, stood within the Love and Light Chariot and held the star tetrahedron crystal in both hands. The angels stood either side of me; first they expanded the star tetrahedron out of my hands and set it around me. Then they formed two more, all three exactly superimposed on each other. Then they twirled and spun them in such a way as to form the saucer-shaped Merkaba Light Body, 'plugging' this into the sacred geometry of the Universe. The Merkaba had been activated. The strange thing was that I did not feel as if

I was moving at all, but a group of stars was now rushing towards me: Ursa Minor, the Little Bear of Seven Stars, Guardian of the Magical Mansion. Suddenly Star Bear herself was behind me, enfolding me in her paws in an aura of violet and white. She was a young polar bear crowned with seven radiant stars and my heart knew that she was also a symbol of the unconditional love of the Christ child. I guessed that her mission was to aid me in opening my own Light centre within to retrieve my lost Divine self. "Yes," she told my heart. "That is my purpose, to offer you this opportunity whilst in this Sacred Space, for this is the spiritual development you can achieve in this Magical Mansion and it is one of the most important places in the quest in terms of future direction."

"Before we go further," she went on, "I need to tell you about what we are about to do. All of mankind's incarnations are designed to perfect the soul's spirituality, through karmic experiences, until that soul is once again in perfect harmony and eventually merges into Oneness with Light. Then that particular soul would have no more need to incarnate. (The soul could still choose to do this, to aid others on their paths, but is not bound to do so.) During any incarnation you can still attain Oneness with All by opening the Angelic Light centre within you. As you guessed earlier, the angels and we animal devas can help you with this. It's the expansion of spiritual consciousness that allows the infinite Love and eternal Light of All to flow both into and from your being. Your actual Angelic Light centre is called the vesica piscis (one of the symbols on the mansion's gate). It's the oval that is created by the overlapping of the Sun and Moon spheres that you've now created within yourself. When you can feel non-judgemental love for yourself you can extend this to Mother Earth and all sentient life in your heart. As you reach out to All, the Divine spark within the vesica piscis ignites with Angelic Light. It begins to radiate Love and Light, and this in turn opens your higher heart, allowing the heart flower to unfold, anchoring this Light within. "Do you understand?" she asked. "I think so," I replied. "Even if you don't then it doesn't matter," she continued, "because subconsciously – in your heart and soul – you do, and at the appropriate time you will also consciously understand. And even if you don't actually see anything on this trip with your human eyes, still it's all happening absolutely as it should!"

"Now if you are ready, we shall depart. You don't need your Merkaba Light Body this time for I shall take you," she announced. "Just sit between my front paws." As I snuggled up to Star Bear the geometry once again formed a Light field around us and we took a right-angle into another dimension. I was in a kind of daze as I found we were travelling on a fast-flowing, spiralling stream that seemed to go in all ways at once. "This is the River of Time," Star Bear told me. Suddenly the River poured over a precipice into sheer nothingness, just dazzling Light lay ahead of us. "The Abyss of Light," said Star Bear, "and you are glimpsing, in a manner your soul can accept, the final destination of the Way of Love and Light."

This Angelic Light was so bright that I could hardly bear to look at it, but contained so much Love that I was entirely filled with Bliss. "Are you sure I don't have to die to experience this Bliss again?" I asked. "No of course not," replied Star Bear, "for this is the Divine Light of which I spoke. It's true that those on their soul journeys in between incarnations will pass some time here, and perfected souls will merge completely with Light, but in any lifetime with enough Love you can carry it within your higher heart. In fact if you complete the final mansion experience it will radiate out from your Heart Flower."

"All you have to do is stand at the edge of the Abyss and ask for this enlightenment. If you have raised your spiritual awareness sufficiently in terms of self-healing and balance, and if your heart wills it to be so in order to be empowered to send Love to others, it will be given to you. Remember that this Light connects you directly to the angels and Oneness with All. When you are heart-centred you can always receive angelic heart and soul guidance during meditation." With loving intent I focused on the power of my will and the wisdom I'd learnt so far during the quest. I asked for Angelic Light to empower my lost Divine self, pledging that I wanted to hold this Light in order to complete the quest and to help others. "You spoke well," exclaimed Star Bear, as a ray of Angelic Light travelled to the vesica piscis within me and I felt this Light instantly radiate throughout my body, shining out from my aura and turning the star tetrahedron around me into dazzling crystalline fire. "I am very proud of you," she growled softly, and hugged me. In the very next breath we found ourselves back in Violet Night, outside the Magical Mansion, whereupon she waved her paw and disappeared.

Chapter 6

Wisdom Mansion of Jupiter
🖌 *Power with Love is the secret Wisdom*

In the corridor once again, outside the mist-wreathed amethyst gate, I paused to allow my eyes to grow accustomed to the pink-lavender light. Then I ventured down the corridor's curve until it abruptly came to an end with a sharp right-angle turn to the left, becoming as dark as midnight. I paused again and it was as well that I did so, as although this next corridor of the labyrinth curved away in front of me I suddenly perceived there was no floor at all – it was just air! There was simply a space, like a lift shaft, except that this space was horizontal rather than vertical. "What do I do now?" I wondered aloud. The sky was once more as normal. A gentle illumination of moon and countless stars shone through a roof of blue-green fluorite onto a floor of glittering starstone. Suddenly, the light fell upon two beautiful mystical Horses that were silently approaching me from around the curve: one was a gleaming blue-black while the other glowed pearly white in the moonlight. Behind them shone the golden chariot I had seen in the last mansion. "If you can name our roles, and the angel for whom we work, we shall help you reach the next mansion," came their words.

As I gladly answered them, "Climb aboard!" they chorused in unison, "for this Light Chariot of Love solves all problems, and we shall convey you to the next gate." As good as their word, we sped for a short distance through the air, round the curve to the left, then not long afterwards we stopped. I was pleased to see that the corridor's floor reappeared in front of the next niche.

Within the niche was a dark wooden gate framed by two great pillars carved from royal blue semi-precious stone flecked with gold. I knew this stone had been revered since ancient times. The gate itself was made of ebony and studded with snakes with golden eyes in strange circular patterns. Once again, flowers were carved into it, and the doorknobs were shells holding the pure geometry of the spiral. The White Horse had disappeared but the Indigo Horse remained. "I am the gatekeeper of this mansion," he informed me. "You have already answered the question about my role; you now need to name two semi-precious stones and

two special symbols of wisdom that may be seen on this gate. If you can answer correctly, I shall give you two gifts you will need during your visit to this mansion."

As I gave the right answers, he tossed his handsome head and dropped into my open hand an ammonite – a fossilised wisdom shell – and also a feather coated in copper; I placed these carefully in the rucksack. Then he lifted one shining hoof and rapped on the gate. At once it opened to reveal the elegant Wisdom Mansion of Jupiter. We both entered the huge, hexagonal, temple-like chamber and the gate closed softly behind us. As I marvelled at the graceful proportions, I saw that at each of the six inner angles of the hexagon there was a pillar, but these seemed merely decorative (or so I thought at the time) for there was no roof. The Wisdom Mansion was open to the deep-blue velvet night sky. The bright full moon shone directly down onto these pillars, casting geometric shadow patterns. Sacred geometry again, I thought.

"As the name implies, you may gain wisdom in this mansion," announced the Indigo Horse. "I await to take you on a route around the six Wisdom Pillars, for you may ride upon my back. Each pillar activates a visual message for you, which can only be obtained when the right key is found and applied."

"But I thought there were Seven Pillars of Wisdom," I objected. "Ah," replied the Horse. "When you have acquired the six pillars' wisdom, you become the seventh yourself." And with this deeply enigmatic remark he knelt down his front legs and I climbed upon his back. As he rose to his feet I saw that it was a long way to the ground. However, though not much of a rider, I was not about to be dissuaded from this part of my adventure.

He walked with proud steps to the first Wisdom Pillar, and soon I perceived that this was of deep red marble. Beneath the pillar was a carved red throne-like chair studded with rubies. It was guarded by the She-Leopard, who lay directly in front of it, and both throne and She-Leopard faced towards the centre of the temple-like chamber. I then noticed that in this centre was a large hexagon-shaped stage. From the Horse's back I looked again at the red marble pillar, wondering how to proceed. Suddenly I saw that level with me there was a small square opening in the red pillar, and in my mind I put together the pieces of the puzzle – red and square. I knew then what I had to do; I searched in the rucksack, extracted the right object and placed it in the cavity of the pillar. I felt, rather than heard, the words: "You have located the correct key. Now dismount, be seated on the Ruby Throne and watch."

I dismounted from the horse and obeyed the instruction, seating myself carefully on the Ruby Throne as the She-Leopard stood aside. On the stage a hologram appeared, showing a succession of scenes in a few seconds. First, a small cottage we had once owned with a magnificent view: I saw myself with my husband and then my two babies appeared. Tears streamed down my face, for I had loved that cottage best of all our homes – it had brought me so much peace, but alas it was not suitable for a growing family. Then I saw a succession of other dwellings, and that my ambition had led to my large current house. I felt my state of stress and poor health resulting from running my business. I felt again that state of having money but no peace of mind. Finally, I was shown another small cottage, again with a wonderful rolling view of fields and trees. "See," said the She-Leopard. "This is your future, if you have the wisdom to choose to follow your true soul path. Your forgiveness has freed you to make this choice." It was so lovely that I cried once again, but this time because of the sheer beauty of the scene. "Here is what was in the box," she continued, and she dropped into my hand a small metal symbol comprising six interlocking circles. "Why, it's the Flower of Life!" I said. "Keep it, for you will need it," she advised; and I placed it into the rucksack.

I mounted the Indigo Horse once again and he took me to the second pillar that was of orange carnelian. Under it was a throne carved and decorated with amber – the Amber Throne – facing the hexagon stage. This time, the Feathered Dragon guarded the throne. Now I knew what I had to do. I searched in the rucksack to find what I needed, and inserted it into the pillar. Once again came the words: "Be seated on the Amber Throne and watch." I dismounted from the Indigo Horse and the Dragon glided to one side as I did as I was told and looked towards the central stage. The hologram showed me studying, reading and worrying about the loss of my business. Next I was in tears because I had no money at all; my husband was most unhappy about the situation, pressing me to seek a job. I was imploring the angels, who had taken me to this point, to show me the way forward. Then I

saw a letter being sent to a publisher, meetings and the scene changed to a large crowd of people, with myself standing on a stage and addressing them. On a table in front of me was a lovely book bound in pale blue and a set of *Harmony Angel Cards*; both bore my name as author. I viewed them in wonder. "All this is possible," promised the Dragon, "for it is what you will achieve if you choose to commit to this new path – your Light Work. Indeed, your transformation has started and will continue, if you show the patience and stamina needed to find the start of this particular path. There are many unsung heroes who are waiting for the knock on the door that never comes. The new beginning will be up to you." I was – unusually – rendered speechless.

For the third time I mounted the Indigo Horse, who trotted to the third Wisdom Pillar. This one was clear quartz and the Throne was pure gold, the sacred metal of the Sun. The Solar Lion, not surprisingly, guarded it and calmly regarded me with his glorious blue eyes. Whilst still on the back of the horse I rummaged for the third object, soon finding it and inserting it into the corresponding aperture in the crystal pillar, which of course it fitted. I dismounted and, now knowing the drill, approached the Sun Throne, the Lion obligingly moving aside. Eagerly, I faced the stage and the third hologram materialised. I saw myself standing beside a person lying on a couch. Angelic healing energy was being channelled through my crown, flowing through my hands and into that person. As it did so my own energy meridian glowed golden; this healing energy radiated around me, healing me at the same time as I tried to heal another. "The more you give, the more you receive, you see," whispered the Lion in my ear. I saw strength and healing flowing into the person on the couch and I knew this was an important aspect of my future role. "Although the hands-on healing is only a means to an end for you," continued the Lion, "it is the way you will get started on your own work which is to open Doors of Light for people, for you care deeply about others." Once again I was too full of emotion to speak and my eyes filled with tears. "But I am not psychic and I don't know if I can channel healing," I protested. "Everyone who wants to heal others can do so abundantly – it's a matter of will and intent," said a new voice in my heart, "and it is part of your Light path."

Now my journey continued to the fourth Wisdom Pillar, and no doubt you've guessed that this pillar was green, carved from malachite. There was a silver throne, studded with moonstones and a huge emerald, and surrounded by green mist; the Dolphin floated in front of it. It was hard to part with the fourth gift, but I inserted it into the green pillar, dismounted and, with Dolphin's permission, seated myself on the Emerald Throne, preparing to watch the hologram. I saw myself immersed in angelology and other ancient wisdom, even back to Lemuria. Then, translating this into twenty-first-century mode, retrieving my own hidden pearl as I put together special angel workshops. From this, I was drawn to visit sites of ancient civilisations, so that I could comprehend that all paths to Truth eventually converge. I saw my husband surprised and dismayed, but unable to stop my explorations; these were both of inner self and then actual travel to places in which he had no interest himself. I perceived he felt threatened by my knowledge, and that the marriage would be severely tested, because each time, when I came back from these trips, I would be greatly changed. Would we stay together or part? It could have gone either way. But then that future cottage was once again shown to me, and we were still together. The voice said: "Your love is deep and you will not be parted."

The Indigo Horse and I now trotted to the fifth Wisdom Pillar, made from angelite – celestial blue and white. I found the right gift and slotted it into a matching cavity in the pillar. The Sapphire Throne was also wreathed in blue mist, guarded by a magnificent Swan, who proudly glided aside as I took my place on it. The hologram started, showing my teenage children and their embarrassment as their former businesswoman mother now began speaking of healing and angels. However, it was obvious that this was my Truth and I had no intention of abandoning it now I had found it. I saw them experiencing healing themselves and becoming converted. My daughter was seen learning it herself; I saw my son with a broken collarbone, and myself giving him healing to speed up his recovery. My husband's spiritual consciousness expanded towards mine and his acceptance grew. All was well. Then the hologram showed a table with many more of my books and card sets on it and with translations into other languages. "See how your work expands," that voice instructed, "like a flower it unfolds across the world. It will help many people so long as you retain that complete integrity symbolised by the Feather of Truth."

Finally the Indigo Horse and I approached the sixth and final Wisdom Pillar in that mansion. I saw that the pillar was of turquoise, a wisdom stone of the Native Americans, while the throne was of precious lapis lazuli, beloved by Ancient Egyptians. I found the gift that I needed and placed it in the round space in the pillar. Then I dismounted and, as the Indigo Horse was the Guardian of this Lapis Throne, he allowed me to be seated upon it. I watched the stage as a picture formed of wonderful geometric patterns, all interlocking. "This is a key to All," spoke the voice in my heart. "You see the Universe resembles a geometric jigsaw, the shapes linked together through the Cosmic Web. Everything in Nature is formed through this geometry, but mankind has forgotten and become separated from All. With the understanding of sacred geometry the link is re-forged and this is how spiritual consciousness truly expands. At each level, first you heal and then you seek spiritual expansion; it is an eternal dance. If you write about this it will resonate with those for whom the message is a wake-up call, and they will learn how to raise their vibration closer to us, to the Creator whom we serve. They will once again join the collective consciousness of All, or you could say, they will find Oneness. This is enlightenment – no separation and mutual respect for All Life. It is a Place of Peace found through the Way of Love and Light, and as Hermes Trismegistos says, it is Wisdom used with Power of Love."

As I remounted the Indigo Horse he headed for the stage in the middle of the chamber, and tossing his head he whinnied: "Here I leave you, for you are becoming the Seventh Wisdom Pillar yourself." As I dismounted and stood tall upon that hexagonal stage, there was a flash of golden Light, threaded with bright turquoise and deep, royal blue, and then the Ruler of Jupiter materialised in all his splendour. "Well done indeed!" was his greeting. "You have successfully finished your mission here, for I have observed you throughout and it was my voice that you heard. It is now time to move on. Your one remaining gift – the contents of the sandalwood box – is for the Place of the Higher Heart. When you get there use it well, and remember – endings are but new beginnings in the eternal spirals of Wisdom."

Chapter 7

Mansion of Mercury & Air
🪶 *Feather and sword point to Truth's path*

Somehow I found myself outside the ebony gate once again. Dawn was breaking, but I now saw with some trepidation that the corridor leading onwards from the Wisdom Mansion was a channel of deep indigo-blue water. Once again, the roof was of crystal, but this time it was of larimar and seemed to capture both rising sun and sky and reflect them down on to the water channel, causing it to sparkle with a luminescent multicoloured light. The corridor curved gently to the left, and of course I didn't know how long it actually was, but while I was pondering on the problem a huge and stately Swan appeared (the one I had seen in the Wisdom Mansion), gliding around the curve towards me. "If you can say what I represent then I can help you get to the next mansion," came the words.

As I gave her the correct answer, she motioned me to climb onto her broad back. The Swan was shaped like a normal bird, but there the resemblance ended, for she was much larger and had translucent feathers that gleamed with their own phosphoresce in the dim light from the crystal roof. It was a very strange journey indeed; I could see the water through her body, and I was completely enveloped in the otherworldly Light of her feathers and the crystal water reflections as we gently proceeded to the end of the indigo corridor. Presently we turned sharply right into the next corridor, and now the sun shone through a blue roof of celestite crystal. I saw that the Swan had a pale blue beak. "Why is your beak blue?" I asked. "Because it is a visual aid to focus you towards linking heart with mind and soaring into the power of the sky. Air is Breath of Life and leads towards Divine Truth," she replied, pointing her beak upwards, where I saw that indeed it was exactly the same colour as both roof and sky. "You will find out more in the Mercury Mansion, for I am its Guardian," she promised. The healing Light and the water's aqua-blue colours soothed and healed me as we glided along the new mystical corridor.

Presently the water channel led us to a great ornamented gate, framed by carved and decorated wooden posts that formed a point above it. This point reflected in the water below

as well, forming a sacred geometric shape. Of pale-grey weathered teak, the posts were carved in a wonderfully delicate way, with vines that entwined around them. Then I noticed that there were also carved symbols of Truth, flowers and creatures representing healing power of Air. The gate itself was faintly Eastern in appearance. It was studded with cornflower-blue sapphires and it was inlaid with myriad tiny mirrors, each of which reflected the Swan's ethereal grace and beauty as well as the sparkling water in which she floated. As she deposited me on the narrow strip of earth immediately in front of the gate she pointed at it with her beak. Then she stated: "If you can tell me the mansion's element, a creature connected with it and then a crystal that is linked, the gate will open." As I answered her, she inclined her graceful neck. The gate swung inwards, causing all the reflections to dance and quiver until I could not see where she finished and the water began. Inside, I glimpsed the shining White Horse and by the time I looked round again the Swan had vanished.

As I entered the mansion the Horse regarded me calmly with large dark eyes. "Well met!" she whinnied. Bathed in bright sunlight was a crystal chamber in the form of a huge octahedron, extending far above as well as below where I stood inside the gate. This one is the Platonic solid for the element of Air, how very appropriate, I thought to myself.

The chamber was divided into upper and lower halves. The upper part of the octahedron was filled with hazy blue, as if somehow it contained the very sky itself, with pure cloudy white at its central top point. Exactly halfway down the octahedron it turned lavender-blue woven with sapphire, then it darkened gradually to cobalt blue. At the very bottom point it became the intense blue of midnight. Vertical, in the exact centre, was what appeared to be a slender beam of bright golden Light, reaching from the octahedron's central lowest point towards its corresponding central point high above in the roof. As I craned my neck to look up, way above me, near the top and encircling the golden beam there was what seemed to be a horizontal circular Light platform. The effect was like a huge rapier-like sword, hilt upwards, and of course I then realised that this was exactly what it was – a Light Sword – whose point disappeared into the midnight-blue light below me. I stood on that threshold wondering how to proceed, while the Horse continued to regard me with her lustrous eyes.

"I want to go up there," I said, pointing to the platform high up in the roof. "First things first," she replied calmly. "That's the spiritual healing point and first you need to address mind and body issues."

Suddenly a mighty being appeared before me, clothed in golden Light rays and radiating beams of varying shades of blue – all those within that chamber and more that I could not name. "Can you tell me the energy centre with which I can especially assist you?" asked the Ruler of Mercury, for of course it was he. As I answered, a second angel materialised, surrounded with palest blue and with pure white Light wings. "And who am I?" he asked. I named him: the Guardian Angel of Spiritual Perception – in this case that of Spiritual Truth, that Truth to which the angels and White Horse could surely lead me.

"Tell me about your Truth," invited Michael. I thought deeply. "The fact is, I am addressing my personal Truth by not restarting my consulting business and instead submerging myself in angelology. I now have the wisdom to see that, though it's quite strange, really, because I am not sure where it's going to lead. I just know I have to continue with it because it's what I am supposed to do. There's been a certain amount of resistance from my husband, because as soon as I started learning healing my consulting business, and therefore my entire income, vanished within a couple of months. But he's going along with my change of direction for the time being because he loves me."

"That is so," acknowledged Michael. "But associated with your past are various blocks in your throat that need to be cut away, and this is the mansion in which to do this. Some date from many years ago, starting from when you were a solitary child who found it difficult to make friends and easier to be alone. Others from when you were unhappy working for your father. And some from the fact that there were things you wish you had said to your parents, but they both died so suddenly that the chance was lost. These are all mind or emotional issues. You suffered from sore throats quite a bit, didn't you?" I admitted that I had. "It was because you suppressed your Truth," he informed me. "The emotional became a physical issue. You've moved beyond some of this, but you can now cut away the last vestiges of any of those issues, for once you've tackled the causes you can remove the remaining effects of

the problems. Raguel and I can aid you to release these types of things, so long as you are not doing anything to hurt another. That is the rule in this mansion and, as you've done all that work in the other mansions, now is the time for you to pledge to speak and live your Truth. Also the element of Air will complete the Moon, Air and Water pyramid within you."

"I'm up for that," I cried. "How do I start?" "Look more closely at the vertical Light Sword and the blue colours in this chamber," commanded Michael. "See where the blue is a mauve shade; from there and above it's Breath of Life – healing power of Air. Do you see a small golden and sapphire platform there?" I focused my eyes and sure enough, there was a little circle to be seen where he pointed, although it was resting on nothing – only thin air. Straight away I knew how to reach it. "Yes," answered Michael, "the White Horse can take you there."

"But I am nervous of heights," I protested. "As you've been told before," replied Michael, "there is nothing to fear in any part of the labyrinth, and we are with you. You will overcome this anxiety if you trust and believe you will."

The Horse knelt down on her two front legs and I climbed upon her glossy back. Then she stood up and, as I clung on to her shining white mane, she took me up and deposited me on the little platform, inside the Light Sword where it held Breath of Life. Cradled by the cool blue-mauve and warm golden Light I found that I felt no fear, for Michael himself hovered beside me. "Now there is something else I must instruct you about," he told me. "The octahedron is a sacred geometry shape. Like everything in Templa Mar and this labyrinth it exists in more than one dimension, and its top and bottom points have special functions. The top point connects inter-dimensionally to the Abyss of Light, while the bottom point carries away negative energy to be transmuted by Mother Earth herself back into Light."

"You need to focus one at a time on the issues you wish to cut away, for you are standing in the power of my Light Sword of Truth. If you truly wish to let go of these, and if it's for your highest good, as you focus on them I will cause the power of the sword to release them." He went on: "I must tell you that fear, depression, unjustified anger, frustration and emotions such as these are all formed from dark negative energy and residues of this will be trapped in your chakra centres. When I help you to release these blocks they will flow down through the base of the octahedron for transmutation. Do you understand me?"

I replied that I understood perfectly, and I set to work determining those things for release, to make the most of this opportunity. There was my remaining lack of self-confidence in my looks and worry about my shortcomings. My anxiety over starting a completely new phase in life and what people would think about angelology, including the loss of my former friends who thought I had gone mad. Whether my husband would continue to support this new way of life and my marriage would survive. Whether we could financially afford for me to do all this. Concerns about the IBS, even though this was now more behavioural programming as I had started healing it. Regrets about my parents, worry that I would inherit my mother's tendency to severe depression; a serious family dispute that needed to be forgiven and forgotten. I realised that there were many issues that I wanted to cut away from myself.

"Right, I am ready," I told Michael, who, true to his Guardianship, was waiting patiently for me. "Then we will begin, and you must breathe in Breath of Life in order to will these negative thoughts to leave you," he ordered.

"Take that Breath of Life and lift your arms up towards the roof of this chamber." And so saying, instead of the beam being around me, the golden Light Sword suddenly seemed to penetrate right through me, starting at my crown, and all those negative energies flowed down through root chakra and away, to disappear through the bottom point of the octahedron. The moment that happened, cobalt blue rays flowed in and through me to cleanse the energy centres where the sword had removed negativity. This was followed by intense sapphire healing rays further brightening my chakra flowers. I saw also that my inner pyramid of Moon, Air and Water over thymus and heart was indeed fully empowered and energy flowed down to lower self, balancing completely the Sun, Earth and Fire pyramid. With this and my Truth pledge I started to rise up the Light Sword – like going up in a sort of Light lift – until I reached the high platform that formed the sword hilt, where Raguel awaited me. He was near the top of the chamber, amid the misty white Light. The four sections of the roof then opened outwards like petals, and a cloud of pure white feathers drifted in to envelop me in a soft cloak. I snuggled into its cosy warmth, watched tenderly by Raguel and Michael. I felt lighter and somehow my energy seemed more refined; and I sensed things clarify in my mind, aiding my ability to communicate more clearly. More than this, though, I perceived my path of spiritual Truth.

"Of course, for this is the Cloud of Knowing," Raguel informed me. "For as you are aware the feather is an ancient symbol of Truth. Now that you have gained in perception you will be aided in moving from your own personal Truth to Absolute Truth, for part of your Soul Journey is to teach others to seek this Truth." The White Horse hovered nearby. "The White Horse will escort you back to the gate, but keep this feather image in your heart always, and look out for tiny white feathers in your path in everyday life, for they are spiritual symbols that guide your steps to the Creator's Absolute Truth."

As I thanked the angels, the White Horse took me gently back down to the mansion gate. I dismounted and hugged her noble neck; she pawed the ground and the gate opened to let me through, back into the corridor. Now, a gentle blue-gold light filtering through a blue topaz roof heralded the approach of dawn again in this part of the labyrinth. Having completed the seventh Mansion of Mercury & Air, I knew that the quest was drawing to a close and that this was the dawn of its final day.

Chapter 8

Place of the Higher Heart
🍂 *Your heart flowers with Beauty, Love and Light*

Somewhat overwhelmed, I now stood on the other side of the Mercury Mansion's gate, fortunately on solid ground. I definitely felt different – lighter, yet at the same time calm, peaceful and centred, and somehow greatly expanded within my heart and soul.

I walked slowly along the now misty blue corridor; presently I reached the end and turned another right angle to my right. As I did so, dawn broke in all its glory and the sun burst through a roof of tourmaline, lighting up the scene. There in front of me was the most magnificent archway I had ever seen. It was made from square blocks of rose quartz, which shone pearl-pink and gold in that dawn light. Set into the top of the arch was a stained-glass panel with a design in copper (the metal of Love) set with rose and emerald; it was exactly like my gift from the She-Leopard – the Flower of Life, the first geometry fractal of healing. The same patterns were woven with gold into the pink-and-green Light wings of a splendid being occupying the arch. On one side of this being was a huge Peacock, whose blue-green feathers shimmered in the light, showing the vesica piscis symbols on his tail. Why, I understand all that now, I mused. On the other side was my old friend of the golden russet coat, the Hound of Heaven. "You've come a very long way since last we met," the Hound commented proudly. The three barred my way, but I was not to be deterred.

"The first step is to name this angel and his Guardianship," stated the Hound. "Absolutely correct," he barked to my answer. "Now, you may only enter this final chamber if it corresponds to your own true heart's desire. Plus your heart must be full of love and your intention honest and true. To ascertain this we need you to tell us firstly what you want to accomplish within this chamber, and secondly what you will do if you achieve your aim."

"Does she speak the Truth?" the angel asked of the two Mystical Animals, as I responded. "Yes," announced the Peacock. "I can see into her heart and crown chakras, and it is a noble and true aim." The Hound looked into my eyes, and thus into my very soul. "Indeed," he replied. "Her intent is pure and honest and she wishes to use what she achieves

to help others find the Way of Love and Light." "Then she may enter," pronounced the angel. That said, they all moved to one side to allow me to enter the final chamber.

"Before you go in, we have a couple of other messages for you," said the Hound. "Mine is to tell you that you've already overcome the blocks in your lower self that stopped you from seeing who you really are – your true self – and being able to love that self despite its faults. So that is excellent progress, especially for a first go at the quest!" "And I just want to say," the Peacock put in, "that when the song of joy and Oneness spirals between your heart and your head, you will know you've completed the quest at this particular level, but feel free to come back when you want to continue to the next one."

Bearing these lovely words in my heart, I entered the chamber that sat at the heart of the labyrinth. It was circular, once again hewn from rose quartz but roofed in translucent kunzite. Through it the rays of the sun lit the interior with palest pink radiance; strangely it also carried the scent of roses. Inside awaited two more great angelic beings: none other than the ruler of Venus, and with her the Heavenly Mother herself. I was intrigued to see that in the centre of the chamber itself was a huge round empty bowl of rose quartz crystal. There were steps up to the rim. Resting on the rim was a cross shape dividing it into four quadrants. Melchisadec's Chalice, I thought to myself, his symbol of finding wholeness. Looking up I saw that the convex ceiling also bore a corresponding cross, but these quadrants were open to the blue sky above.

"That's right," acknowledged Haniel. "It's in the form of Melchisadec's Key. You have sensed this chamber throughout the quest, and now you've arrived here. The fragrance of roses is connected with angels, unconditional love and, of course, heart. This chamber is also called the Place of the Higher Heart. It exists simultaneously as both Macrocosm (connected to the heart of Mother Earth herself and from there to All) and Microcosm (to the heart of the seeker of Eternal Truth). In Macrocosm it resonates with all similar planetary hearts at Galactic and Universal levels, while in Microcosm the link is with other open human hearts. Not only is it a place of immense healing, but also of the potential for pure and limitless expansion of spiritual self, a connection that starts and finishes at the Abyss of Light. You must remember that since your experience in the Mansion of Pluto you now have an Angelic Light centre – vesica piscis – within your higher heart, the first step to Unity Consciousness."

"However, there are some things you do not yet fully understand," she went on. "Spirituality is not the sole prerogative of religion (although it could be if you want it to be and provided it does not enslave you). But really spirituality is about having a heart that is truly open to Love and Light every minute of every day. Spiritual consciousness is realising that you are part of All, it's respecting All – particularly all sentient life – and wanting to help heal All with unconditional love. This includes the animal kingdom, all of nature and even the earth and rocks. Everything that holds memories can be called sentient and should also be given respect. It's the very separateness of mankind that has caused the troubles of your world, for if every human felt part of the collective consciousness and had this Love to send out, emanating from a higher heart full of Light, then how could you have wars to kill and maim others? Understanding this in heart and soul is called Enlightenment."

Pistis Sophia took up the story: "What you need to know is that through your heart and soul you can dream a new reality and actually start to manifest it – not just who you really are but also the reality of a peaceful Earth. Then through connecting with other similar human hearts, as you use the power of Love to send out healing from your own healed and balanced higher heart of Light, it all magnifies exponentially and will actually birth this new, expanded reality for All. Your healing can go to all sentient life, for even negative thought forms can linger and need healing or transmuting back to Light. Not to mention soul fragments – either your own or those of others you've lost but still cling on to; then this transmuted Light just combines with the Love to reinforce that wonderful new reality you dreamed. Also, in the same way as you experienced in the Mansion of Moon, Neptune & Water, the healing you send is always magnified before being returned to you with great gratitude. And that's why you feel Bliss. Other quests can build on your skills in this regard."

"Finally, the very fact that you want to send out this healing continuously transforms you by raising your consciousness, further aiding your personal spiritual development towards Oneness. So, in this chamber obstacles can be overcome and you can start to rewrite your

personal template in the Stars," Pistis Sophia went on. "All you need is enough faith and trust, and combined Love, Power and Wisdom, to believe that you can do it. One more vital thing to understand is that the Flower of Life is not just a pretty pattern, but a healing geometry that works both in Macrocosm and Microcosm, as will shortly become clear to you. For sacred geometry is the form behind All, and underpins dreaming and manifesting this new reality; thus it is crucially important for what is termed Heart and Earth Ascension. This is all we have to say at present, for it is no use us just telling you, you have to experience the feeling for yourself. Now you need to reach that platform and then ask your heart how to open your own heart flower – Love is the Key."

These words, the rosy light and the fragrance of roses enveloped and filled me with warmth and happiness. I climbed the steps up to the high rim of Melchisadec's Chalice and looked within. It was empty. The metal cross that was balanced on the rim was made of fine tubes of the seven Sacred Metals bound together. Over the centre of this cross was a large beaten copper circle and mounted on this was a square of emerald. On that was a triangle of seven alexandrites (a stone of heart alchemy). This whole centrepiece platform rested on a plinth rising from the base of the chalice, but I could see no way to reach it, as I was not about to crawl along the metal cross. I knew that I must reach the centrepiece and then I realised how to get there. "Thunderbird, Thunderbird, Thunderbird," I called. "Please come and take me to the emerald couch, in Love and Light, Love and Light, Love and Light." Thunderbird immediately appeared. "If you can tell me the seven metals forming the cross, I will take you to its centre," she sang.

Of course I could and did tell her. Motioning me onto her snow-white back, she flew me to the central copper circle and deposited me on the square emerald within its alexandrite triangle. I sat down and reflected on the fact that the wisdom of Hermes Trismegistos was inscribed on Emerald Tablets and on the sacred geometry of the shapes. I thought about how to proceed. Pistis Sophia had told me that the Flower of Life was connected with the puzzle. I suddenly knew what to do. Remembering my gift of a Flower of Life symbol, I retrieved it from my knapsack.

Haniel had mentioned the importance of the vesica piscis within me – my own Light centre in my higher heart. I focused my expanded psychic senses onto the spheres of Sun and Moon within me and my vesica piscis of Angelic Light. I was aware of the Light that now filled it but intuited that there was more to be done. With mind, body and spirit I sought clarification on my next step. Instantly I received it. I held the Flower of Life within my hands, and with all my heart and soul, and loving will and intent, I focused on this symbol, asking for it to become part of me. Through the cross above me, open to the sky, I asked to connect to the Sun. Then I breathed in the crystalline Light of Cosmic Spirit, the Breath of the Creator. Acting as a conduit between Earth, Sun and Stars I asked to magnify this with the power of my own Light centre, and on the out breath I sent it down through the cross beneath me to Mother Earth's heart. Then, as the crystalline energy returned from the heart of Mother Earth through me en route back to the Sun, a kind of miracle occurred. Instead of just the Sun and Moon spheres within me it inscribed others to form six spheres – a crystal Flower of Life with Angelic Light radiating from each petal at its heart.

Now, through the four quadrants of the open roof, poured Water of Life in silver and blue and aqua healing spirals, filling the chalice beneath me with sparkling radiance. I saw that the Flower of Life within me was a three-dimensional hologram of Love and Light and I sent this out to the waters in the chalice to help heal Mother Earth. Then the Water of Life ceased, and that bright golden star, our Sun, beamed Fire of Life spirals into the chamber, onto my body, so I sent the healing holograms out again to heal the Sun, source of Life. Finally I breathed Breath of Life and I sent healing holograms also to the Air. Each time, the magnified healing returned to my own heart. And when at last I looked within myself, at the green water-lily bud that I had cleansed in the Mansion of Neptune and Moon (aeons ago) a beautiful magenta-pink lily had opened in my higher heart.

Now I understood what Pistis Sophia, and indeed Melchisadec and Hermes Trismegistos, had meant, because I could sense that the pattern or mandala of the Flower of Life healed at mind, body and spirit levels. It now not only flowed into and through my very blood as Microcosm, but also at the same time, as Macrocosm it radiated out in healing fractals and holograms of pure Love and Light from my higher heart to All. From my experience in the Cloud of Knowing in the Mercury Mansion I knew that this was the Creator's Truth. Through my opened heart flower, and by willing and intending a new Reality of Peace through Love and Light to emanate from it, I could raise the vibration of Mother Earth and all her life forms. And by doing so my heart would be in resonance with all other open hearts helping to manifest this reality, and it was this that would bring me an indescribable sense of belonging, of joy and of bliss. Indeed, this joy then spiralled in golden Flower of Life patterns around my entire body and I realised the meaning of the Peacock's last remark to me. I also knew beyond any doubt that the Way of Love and Light had changed me forever.

Thanks to the angels, and to my commitment to it, the Quest of the Heart was now completed. In an instant the vision faded and, though I did not wish to depart, the visit to Templa Mar was over.

With a smile on my face I opened my eyes to find myself lying on my bed at home, once again in this life and in this space. The external reality appeared the same as before, but all else had changed, for I was transformed and in a state of inner peace; my core values redefined and my new reality dreamed. Of course at times it would be difficult to sustain that smile, to keep the faith and manifest those dreams. But I knew that now I had found the Way to Oneness with All, and with the power of Love and Light flowering within my higher heart, the quest memories were part of me. I could regenerate my experience any time through meditation. And moreover, I couldn't wait to start it all over again....

Heed well the Law of Three relating to All
with Angels, Sacred Geometry and
the Way of Love and Light.
For Sacred Geometry is
the Eternal Truth behind the form of All,
Love and Light are the powers that bind All, and
Angels guard and guide us along the Way to Oneness with All.

The
Angel Quest
Journal

A workbook with meditations

Quest Journal

A word about your quest

The quest's precept: I pledge to show others the Way

I hope you enjoyed my Angel Quest of the Heart narrative. Of course this is a personal account, and I have described it thus. I assure you it all happened to me, although it actually unfolded over the course of about a year during daily meditations, rather than in one continuous sequence. I portrayed it as one story to make it more cohesive, easier to read and absorb, and in a format that I hope may inspire you.

The experiences in the quest were a quantum spiritual leap for me. I should point out that, as in the grail quests of ancient times, even to take part in such a quest is to undertake a kind of pilgrimage. In other words, you are working directly with the spiritual forces of Love and Light to self-heal, but even more importantly, contributing to healing Mother Earth and all her sentient life.

Meditation is not the only way to do such a quest, of course, but it is a method of harmonising mind, body and spirit. The angelic meditations in this journal, combined with the artworks and mandalas, connect you directly to angelic realms. They will take you straight into your heart, linking from there to your soul, enabling safe channelling of angelic guidance. When you invoke the support of Guardian Angels and Mystical Animal Guides, they will protect you throughout these meditations, helping you to ground and process your experiences. This is their role, for you are growing with Love towards Light.

As I have written before, the more you work with angels, the more your vibration will rise, bringing you closer to them so you will gradually sense more. However, it does require patience and a pledge to work at it, as I did, for at first I had no psychic senses to speak of. By committing to the angels these senses developed gradually for me and continue to do so.

MAKE YOUR OWN SPIRITUAL ALCHEMY HAPPEN!

In this journal you are offered the opportunity to take part, in fact to star in your own story – your own Angel Quest of the Heart. It may or may not turn out to be similar to mine. This does not matter in the slightest – the narrative was my journey and yours will be entirely personal to you. You may see what I saw, or you may experience something entirely different, there are no absolutes, no rights and wrongs. If you 'see' nothing (in other words you are not clairvoyant) you may experience the quest through your other psychic senses – for instance you might smell a fragrance, sense energy around or within (clairsentience), or hear a message in your head while meditating (clairaudience). All represent psychic development.

Even if you are not aware of any of this happening, please accept my assurance that you are in fact in the Templa Mar Labyrinth and the healing of mind, body and spirit is taking place. Just trust, and surrender to the experiences. What really matters is that your connection with the angels starts your own journey of spiritual transformation. I strongly suggest you begin at the beginning, as the entire quest builds slowly to its climax and conclusion. Remember, this is your special chance to self-heal and, by allowing the angels' alchemy to work on your heart and soul, to travel on the Way of Love and Light.

The quest experience leads you towards the finding of inner peace. As the angels tell you, you can do the quest and these meditations many times over. If you are pledged to raise spiritual awareness and consciousness, when you clear one level of blocks in your energy system, you will reach the next level and can begin again. It is the role of the angels to support mankind in this spiritual work, as exemplified by such quests, with their unconditional love and to ensure that you are never alone on the Way of Love and Light.

FINDING THE WAY: HOW TO BEGIN YOUR QUEST

🖢 THE TEMPLA MAR AND HEALING MANSION MEDITATIONS: Only try one meditation at a time. I suggest you start with the Templa Mar introductory meditation and then progress through each of the mansions, as I did. You may choose to go through all of them one at a time, or re-do the same one to gain more and more benefit before moving on to the next, or even do just part of a meditation at a time – that choice is yours. Before you start each meditation, determine what relevant issues of your own need addressing (see pages 62–3) while you are in that particular mansion.

Blank pages are provided after each meditation. Use these to note down your answers and your own healing needs to create your personal 'aide memoire' for that particular mansion. When you have finished the meditation, write down your experiences while they are vivid in your mind. You will gradually build upon this as your spiritual consciousness expands, and if you keep re-doing the quest this process will continue to higher and higher levels.

🖑 QUESTIONS AND ANSWERS: Before you start each meditation, re-read the introduction or relevant chapter in my Angel Quest of the Heart narrative. The story contains questions I had to answer during my own quest. Now read the meditation in this journal that relates to that chapter, and you will see that before you start you also need to find some answers, thus demonstrating to the angels your commitment to doing it right, so that you can gain the maximum benefit from it. All the information you need for the quest – derived from ancient wisdom of angelology, plus angelic guidance I have personally received – is provided somewhere in this work, either in my story or in the Angelic Information on pages 62–4 of this journal. But it is key to the quest that you find this information for yourself.

🖑 THE ILLUSTRATIONS: All the illustrations are most important, as they create subliminal Light windows for you to connect to the Guardian Angels and Mystical Animal Guides. The trace pictures at the start of each chapter of my story depict all the beings of that mansion. The gate artworks show important and relevant symbols, and the illustrations showing you the interior chamber of each mansion offer you a composite of the healing that is possible.

The mandala that accompanies each meditation should be viewed for about 30 seconds before starting the meditation, as this actually raises the spiritual awareness needed to reach that mansion and complete this part of the quest.

🖑 INVOKING ANGELS AND MYSTICAL GUIDES: Practise invoking the Guardian Angels and Mystical Animal Guides in the recommended way (see page 7) before you start your quest as they will protect you and guide your quest for your highest good.

Preparing for your quest

PRELIMINARY STEPS

If you are experienced in meditation you will already be aware of some of these points. However, those of you who are relatively new to the art of meditation might like some brief instructions before getting started. Ensure that you are warm enough, sitting comfortably, or if you prefer, lying down. Try not to be disturbed for at least 30 minutes.

- Read the introduction or chapter of the quest narrative to identify the questions you need to answer in order to progress to the next stage.
- Take the trouble to find the answers (all are in the Angel Quest of the Heart narrative or the charts and guides at the back of this book), for this demonstrates commitment to the quest. You are offering this gift of your time and effort to the angels in return for the spiritual experience that will unfold for you throughout the quest.
- Write the answers down in advance to help you to remember them subconsciously.
- Determine the energy centre (chakra) represented in each mansion and any personal issues you want to address in your own corresponding chakra (see page 63), so you can enlist the angels' special assistance.
- View in turn all the artworks for the mansion, including the mandala for the meditation you are about to undertake, as these will aid your angelic connection.
- Then from your heart with loving intent invoke the Guardian Angels and Mystical Animal Guide involved with the mansion, asking them to protect you during this quest experience, ensuring all that happens is for your highest good.
- Allow the angel energy to surround you (usually felt in hands, head, body).
- State, from your heart, that you have committed to the quest, you know all the answers needed to be allowed through the gate and you deserve to be aided to experience fully the mind, body and spirit healing within.
- Before you start each meditation, begin with the following process:

PRE-MEDITATION PROCESS

🐦 With eyes closed, start taking really deep breaths of pure white energy – this is Angelic Light, or Spiritus Dei – the breath of the Creator.

🐦 As you breathe in Angelic Light, breathe it right down into your body, holding the breath as long as is comfortable for you.

🐦 As you breathe out, let go of as many negative emotions as you can (such as fear, depression, anger, sadness) until you start to feel relaxed.

🐦 When you feel filled with Angelic Light, send it down through your toes into Mother Earth; the angels help you direct it to her blue crystalline heart.

🐦 Your Light will connect to the crystal at Mother Earth's heart and she will respond by sending you sapphire-blue energy that you can draw back up through your toes and into your energy meridian from root chakra right up to your crown.

🐦 Weave the sapphire blue into the white Angelic Light within you and send this combined energy to the Sun, giver of life, to send gratitude.

🐦 Now send it beyond to the stars so that you are even now part of All, connected to the Cosmic Web of Life, Love and Light. Enjoy this feeling.

🐦 Now start to breathe the Angelic Light into a bubble around you.

🐦 Visualise this bubble extending into a tunnel of bright Light – white interwoven with blue – which transcends both time and space.

🐦 It does not matter whether or not you can see it, just know it is there.

🐦 When you are ready, ask the angels to accompany your spirit along this Light tunnel, knowing that your body is safely protected and that when the experience is concluded you will return to it.

🐦 At the end of the Light tunnel you will see a circle of coloured light – as you exit you will be at the mountain or outside the mansion gate you seek.

🐦 Now continue with the specific quest meditation that you wish to do.

🖝 When you've completed your mansion experience thank the angels for their loving help and for the healing you received; ask them to close and seal your energy centres if appropriate, opening your eyes when ready.

🖝 As soon as you've opened your eyes, use the blank workbook pages that immediately follow the meditation to note down your experience.

🖝 Also write down any gift you were given by the beings.

If you asked during the meditation for the angels to confer on you any ability to channel healing, test this on yourself, a friend, loved one or pet (pets are usually particularly receptive). Gentle warmth will flow from your palms; trust and work at it. Angels rejoice in empowering mankind to heal.

Remember that each meditation offers you angel alchemy, leading to a new beginning at many different levels. Make the most of this opportunity, bearing in mind that to integrate and process angelic wisdom can take a little time.

HOW TO INVOKE ANGELS AND MYSTICAL ANIMALS

The actual invocation is very simple. Call the angel by name three times. Then ask this angel to be with you, completing your invocation with the words In Love and Light three times, showing that your intent is honest and from your heart. The more you do this, the easier it gets, the more you will feel and the closer in vibration you will become to the angels.

For example, to connect to the angel Raphael: *Raphael, Raphael, Raphael, please be with me now In Love and Light, Love and Light, Love and Light.*

To connect to Raphael's Solar Lion: *Raphael, Raphael, Raphael, I ask to connect through you to the Solar Lion, to open my solar chakra to healing in Love and Light, Love and Light, Love and Light.*

Adapt as necessary.

The Angels ask you to remember: Love is the key.

I pledge to show others the Way

Before starting, follow the pre-meditation process on page 6.

🍂 At the end of the Light tunnel is a circle of blue sky. Emerge in the sunshine near the top of the mountain that leads to finding your true self.

🍂 The Hound of Heaven is beside you to help you to the summit.

🍂 Stand on the summit, seeing woods far below you. Thunderbird appears; she will lead you down the mountain path into the quiet and peaceful woods and beyond these woods to Templa Mar, the eternal Temple of Healing.

🍂 The Guardian Angel of Trees will give you strength if you can name him.

🍂 The Guardian Angel of Nature's Secrets shows you the seven chakra flowers that you can heal in Templa Mar if you complete the quest. Can you name her and these flowers?

🍂 As the trees thin you suddenly see an awe-inspiring sight – a glittering marble and crystal temple that floats in swirling mists of green-and-violet light above the ground. It's Templa Mar, which exists throughout time.

🍂 The angel Roshel awaits you. If you can name her guardianship responsibilities she will let you climb the Light Ladder to the entrance of Templa Mar, for she is the guardian of something you are seeking.

🍂 Climb the Ladder and stand outside the great oaken outer gates, decorated with symbols relating to the quest you are undertaking.

🍂 Two of the quest's ruling angels materialise – can you name these angels and their roles?

🍂 One of these, your spiritual director, Ruler of Sacred Seven, wishes you to name his Sacred Seven angels, with their days, planets and key attributes, as they are all involved in the quest.

🍂 The second mighty being, who offers you spiritual alchemy, wishes you to state how many paths there are for the soul, and how many mansions this quest features?

🍂 These two beings then cause the outer gates to open and you are allowed to enter the first courtyard; this is paved in black and white marble, with fragrant white flowers in pewter planters and an olive tree.

🍂 If you can name the angel (one of the Sacred Seven) whose courtyard this is, he leads you to the labyrinth quest's first corridor.

🍂 The rest will be up to you!

🍂 If you complete the quest, what is your pledge?

Notes

Ignite Healing Sun within & All becomes possible

Before starting, follow the pre-meditation process on page 6.

🌿 At the end of the Light tunnel is a circle of bright sunlight. Emerge in the crystal corridor in front of the Healing Mansion of the Sun.

🌿 Stand before the Solar Lion gatekeeper and answer questions about the ruling angel, flower and energy centre of this mansion.

🌿 If you can say what his ankh represents, the Lion will give it to you to use to unlock the gate.

🌿 The gate opens; the Lion escorts you into the circular crystal mansion.

🌿 Enter the inner quartz crystal pyramid; Raphael and Gazardiel are there.

🌿 Lie down on the crystal couch. Focus on your solar chakra.

🌿 Raphael causes a ray of liquid Sun healing to spiral down through the pyramid into a golden bowl.

🌿 Gazardiel pours this Sun energy into your solar chakra and a miniature Sun forms within you, around this chakra. Light radiates out from it into your body.

🌿 Know that this Sun is the centre of your will and intent. If you really empower this energy centre with Love and Light, All is possible.

🌿 Now the Lion places a small crystal fire pyramid on your solar chakra.

🌿 Raphael causes a rainbow to form over you, the seven rainbow chakra flowers appear and merge into your own body; they are translucent.

🌿 Now, will and intend that your Sun energy heals the solar chakra.

🌿 See the flower on the solar chakra becoming brighter and clearer, radiating its own energy.

🌿 Focus on other issues you know you need Raphael to help you address. See Sun healing taking place and those flowers becoming more distinct.

🌿 Next, visualise your own fire pyramid taking shape within your lower self.

🌿 Will and intend that energy to flow through your fire pyramid's apex and up to start cleansing and purifying your heart.

🌿 If you will it to be so and ask from your heart, Raphael can empower you with some healing ability with which to aid others.

🌿 In a burst of bright Light the Phoenix appears to tell you this is a new beginning, one of many you can and will experience within the quest. The choice, however, is yours.

🌿 The Lion gives you a parting gift as you leave the mansion. Do you accept it?

🌿 Thank these beings for your healing, knowing that All is now possible.

Notes

Transformation through passion and alchemy

Before starting, follow the pre-meditation process on page 6.

❧ At the end of the Light tunnel is a circle of honey-coloured light. Emerge in the crystal corridor in front of the Mansion of Uranus & Fire.

❧ The Dragon gatekeeper asks questions about the ruling angel, flower, energy centre and a symbol of this mansion.

❧ The gate opens and you enter the amber mansion, shaped like a giant hollow egg.

❧ Steps lead up towards a platform in the centre of the egg.

❧ Ask from your heart for the Phoenix to come and guide you through blue-white fire to the platform (your crucible for transformation).

❧ The Phoenix says that this is Fire of Life and cannot harm you, so walk through the flames to the white platform and lie down upon it.

❧ Uriel takes a white ember and passes it along your energy centres, releasing fear of change that may be blocking all chakras.

❧ Now he says: 'Will in the blue-white fire to empower your transformation.'

❧ As you do this, the fire pyramid you started to create within you while in the Sun Mansion becomes stronger, and radiates power upwards.

❧ Now Nathaniel appears, offering you orange fire of passion in the sacral chakra, for whatever you need – life, sexuality, change or all of these.

❧ Mentally ask for the passion you need, and Nathaniel causes orange fire to pour into your sacral centre to fill you with this passion.

❧ Uriel reappears with the Cosmic Tuning Fork, strikes it and holds it against the crucible, vibrations ripple into your sacral chakra; really will this to be healed and harmonised.

❧ Focus on any other energy centres that you know need realigning.

❧ Uriel strikes the tuning fork again and different vibrations ripple through you, changing as they go, so that other chakra centres benefit.

❧ The Cosmic Tuning Fork can harmonise you with Mother Earth's vibration, the Solar System, Galaxy and Universe; ask when you feel you are ready.

❧ The Dragon escorts you back through the gate to the labyrinth, reminds you to keep working towards Unity Consciousness (Oneness with All), and gives you a gift.

❧ Thank the beings for your transformational experience in this mansion.

Notes

Courage & forgiveness allow security and empowerment

Before starting, follow the pre-meditation process on page 6.

➤ At the end of the Light tunnel is a circle of pale red and white light. Emerge in the crystal corridor in front of the Mansion of Mars & Earth.

➤ Stand before the She-Leopard gatekeeper and answer questions about the ruling angel, flower, energy centre and metal of this mansion.

➤ The gate opens and Camael welcomes you into the mansion's square chamber. The roof is pink coral and it confers a warm, rosy light.

➤ In the centre is a plinth on which, at eye level, stands a bowl of flames.

➤ The flames are many shades of red for mind, body and spirit healing.

➤ Mumiah firstly offers you healing of the body: energy and wellbeing.

➤ Step up to the bowl and breathe in ruby flames, filled with diamond sparkles, drawing them right down to the red flower in your root chakra.

➤ Look within and see this flower becoming much brighter, radiating energy both down to your feet and up to your other energy centres.

➤ Now breathe in purple-red flames, with Ariel, who helps these rays flow right through you, strengthening both your connections to Earth and Sun, as well as grounding and balancing you.

➤ Next Camael asks you to address any forgiveness issues you have, either with others or perhaps with yourself. Do you vow to resolve these issues?

➤ If so, breathe deeply of the crimson-magenta flames in the bowl and ask the angels to bring forward and manifest the essence of anybody needing your forgiveness, giving it a form you can recognise.

➤ Even if you don't see these forms, know they are there.

➤ Offer your forgiveness and mentally embrace the form(s) with Love.

➤ Accept any gifts you are now given, safe in the knowledge that by the power of Love and Light and this act of forgiveness you have freed yourself from blocks this caused and truly moved on spiritually.

➤ You have now fully empowered the energy pyramid of Sun, Earth and Fire that you constructed in your lower self, and the power is flowing upwards to help heal and open your personal heart chakra.

➤ She-Leopard escorts you back through the gate to the labyrinth itself.

➤ Thank the beings for security and empowerment gained in this mansion.

Notes

Moon gifts Hope and water bring Tranquillity

Before starting, follow the pre-meditation process on page 6.

🐦 At the end of the Light tunnel is a circle of cool green and aqua light. Emerge in the crystal corridor by the Mansion of Moon, Neptune & Water.

🐦 Stand before the Dolphin gatekeeper and answer his question on the two ruling angels, a crystal of the moon and a crystal called 'water of the sea'.

🐦 Dolphin asks you to be clear on your needs in this mansion, then invites you to swim under the Water Gate with him, holding on to his flipper.

🐦 The crystal mansion is an icosahedron that holds an inverted pyramid, its top open to the Moon, half filled with green-aqua water.

🐦 You stand on a crystal bridge that extends into the pyramid.

🐦 Below you are six floating semi-circular platforms around a floating selenite island; this is a kind of translucent bowl open at top and side.

🐦 The two ruling angels hover over the selenite sphere and await you; there is a scent of lilies in the air and moonlight makes a path for you.

🐦 Dolphin guides you; jump into the water and swim to the selenite sphere.

🐦 Enter and lie down on a green couch within; see the bright Moon above.

🐦 Gabrielle causes a spiral of silver Moon energy to flow down into your personal heart, creating a miniature Moon within you, overlapping the Sun.

🐦 Really will this to bring you hope, self-belief and feminine balance.

🐦 Phuel creates a funnel of moonbeams through which healing Water of Life flows down on you, cleansing your heart of past hurts and brightening the green lily bud and leaves in your personal heart chakra.

🐦 Will the silver and aquamarine energy to form a Moon, Air and Water pyramid within you, flowing down into heart and any energy centres needing emotional healing; feel peace and tranquillity.

🐦 Now the angels ask you to send healing from your heart back to the Water of Life.

🐦 Send Love and Light out from your heart to the Water of Life; it empties through the point of the pyramid to Mother Earth, constantly refilling as fountains spray from the platforms.

🐦 As you swim back under the Water Gate, Dolphin too feels some healing from you, and offers you a parting gift.

🐦 Thank all the beings for their help, enjoying a feeling of calmness and tranquillity.

Notes

Angelic Light Magic illumines your heart

Before starting, follow the pre-meditation process on page 6.

🖐 At the end of the Light tunnel is a circle of pink-lavender light. Emerge in the crystal corridor in front of the Magical Mansion of Pluto.

🖐 Stand before Ariel, who asks which elements does he rule and what are the four symbols on the gate?

🖐 Smoky violet, purple and white mists swirl around the gate; in its centre is a huge, faceted amethyst crystal that has stars in its depths.

🖐 Ariel asks if you wish to go into the crystal, for this forms his mansion.

🖐 Will and intend from your heart that you go into this beautiful crystal to explore our whole universe as well as touch other realities.

🖐 There is an amethyst couch within; Ariel invites you to lie on this couch.

🖐 As you do so, he places smoky quartz and amethyst crystals on you.

🖐 Then, according to your needs, he causes different shades of violet fire to cleanse and purify your chakras, particularly the third eye.

🖐 Say: 'I channel the power of Violet Fire that brings the purity I desire' to help your healing.

🖐 The Sun, Earth, Fire and Moon, Air, Water pyramids within you can now overlap to form a six-pointed star allowing Melchisadec to offer you a star path.

🖐 Using the sacred geometry star within you the angels create a Light Body vehicle around you and you travel to Ursa Minor, where Star Bear of the Violet Night awaits to take you further.

🖐 Between the paws of Star Bear you fly along the River of Time to view the Abyss of Light, so bright that it dazzles all the senses.

🖐 This is Divine Light of Unity Consciousness, but you have the potential to hold this in heart and crown if you have achieved sufficient masculine-feminine and physical-spiritual balance within to third eye level; the six-pointed star within you shows if you have attained this degree of balance.

🖐 Where your own Sun and Moon spheres overlap is your vesica piscis. The angels can transform this into your Angelic Light Centre of Divine Self.

🖐 If you truly wish to help others, to serve All through the power of Love and Light, then the angels will allow Angelic Light to pour into this vesica piscis.

🖐 Now will and intend this – the first step to opening your higher heart – and return holding Angelic Light within your heart, a mighty step to Oneness.

🖐 Thank all the beings for your experiences in the Magical Mansion.

Notes

Power with Love is the secret Wisdom

Before starting, follow the pre-meditation process on page 6.

- At the end of the Light tunnel is a circle of deep blue light, lit by moon and stars. Emerge in the corridor in front of the Wisdom Mansion of Jupiter.
- Stand before Rikbiel's Indigo Horse, the gatekeeper; answer his questions about two crystals and two symbols connected with this particular mansion.
- Enter the huge hexagonal mansion, a Wisdom Pillar stands in each angle.
- Mount the Indigo Horse, who will take you to each Wisdom Pillar in turn.
- The Wisdom Pillars are in rainbow colours, with a matching throne in front.
- There is a hexagonal stage in the centre of the temple-like mansion.
- At the Red Pillar ask the She-Leopard if you may sit on the Ruby Throne. Request the angels to show you what you need to do to further heal this chakra for courage and security in life.
- Note this well; the angels may give you a gift to facilitate this process.
- The Horse now takes you to the Orange Pillar. Ask the Dragon to allow you to sit on the Amber Throne, and be shown by the angels how to continue your life transformation that has started during this quest. As before, note what you are shown and any gifts you are given.
- Go to the Yellow Pillar and sit on the Golden Throne with the Solar Lion's permission. Ask the angels to show you how to continue mind, body, spirit healing; keep the information carefully in your heart.
- Proceed to the Green Pillar, ask Dolphin to allow you onto the Emerald Throne. The angels will show you the next steps in healing heart and emotions, loving and respecting yourself: key spiritual steps.
- Now travel to the Blue Pillar; the Swan can give you permission to sit on the Sapphire Throne. You seek Truth and you have come far, so now see what to do next to move forwards towards personal and Absolute Truth.
- The Indigo Horse takes you to the Indigo Pillar and allows you to sit on the Lapis Throne. Zadkiel tells you Wisdom comes only when Power is used with Love; this is the meaning of the crown of Hermes Trismegistos.
- When you have understood this within heart and mind, then you have found the Way.
- Stand tall on the stage as you become the Seventh Pillar of Wisdom.
- Remember to thank all the beings for their help, guidance and gifts.

Notes

Feather & sword point to Truth's path

Before starting, follow the pre-meditation process on page 6.

🍂 At the end of the Light tunnel is a circle of pale blue light. Emerge in the crystal corridor that becomes a channel of water.

🍂 A Swan glides towards you. If you can name her role, she will take you to the Mercury Mansion.

🍂 Climb on the back of the Swan; her blue beak focuses you towards Truth.

🍂 As you reach the mansion, she says the gate will open if you know the element, a crystal and a creature connected with it; then she disappears.

🍂 The gate opens and you are greeted by Rikbiel's White Horse. Name her role.

🍂 The mansion is an octahedron filled with shades of blue, with white at the top, then lavender, sapphire, cobalt and midnight blue at the bottom point.

🍂 In the exact centre is a slender golden Light Sword (made of Light beams) with its hilt uppermost, in the top point of the mansion's roof.

🍂 Can you name the ruler of Mercury, who then appears?

🍂 He invites you to state what you feel to be your Truth, as clarified in the Jupiter Mansion, and what needs to be cut away to allow you to live it.

🍂 The White Horse takes you to a tiny sapphire platform halfway up the Light Sword; stand on that platform while Michael hovers to protect you.

🍂 Breathe in Breath of Life and with heart and will, ask for the power of the Light Sword to cut away from you those things that need to be released.

🍂 Immediately the golden beam will flow right through you, taking away and down those negative issues to be transmuted to Light through the octahedron's lowest point, freeing your throat and other chakras.

🍂 Cobalt cleanses you, sapphire rays heal and brighten your chakra flowers.

🍂 As you are now lighter, the platform rises up to the viewing area that forms the hilt of the Light Sword and the roof of the mansion opens outwards.

🍂 Raguel causes a cloud of white feathers of Truth to float down and surround you, filling your heart and soul with an inner knowing.

🍂 Raguel tells you that the white feather is always a symbol of Spiritual Truth, and that more feather signs will be given to you on how to keep working towards finding your Truth. For this is the path to Absolute Truth.

🍂 Thank all the beings for their guidance and for your mansion experience.

Notes

Your heart flowers with Beauty, Love and Light

Before starting, follow the pre-meditation process on page 6.

- At the end of the Light tunnel is a circle of pastel pink woven with green. Emerge in the crystal corridor in front of a magnificent arch of rose quartz.
- The arch is embellished with the Flower of Life, in emerald, pink and gold.
- In front of the arch are Pagiel and two Mystical Animal Guardians. To gain entry, can you state the roles of these three beings and your pledge on completing the quest?
- They also say that you must truly wish to help All Life in order to enter here.
- The chamber is hewn from rose quartz, roofed in kunzite; in the centre is a huge chalice-like bowl. Over this is a cross formed of seven sacred metal strands.
- In the centre of the cross is a circular, beaten copper platform surmounted by a square of gleaming emeralds; within this is a triangle of alexandrites.
- Steps lead up to the edge of the bowl, but you must get to the centrepiece.
- If you can name the seven metals that form the cross, you can invoke Thunderbird to fly you to the copper platform; then sit in the triangle.
- Pistis Sophia and Haniel have explained that to open the flower in your higher heart is to attain Oneness and thus to be able to dream a new reality for yourself, as well as ground and manifest it to aid Mother Earth and all her life forms.
- The Flower of Life is a key to accomplish this; you already have your Angelic Light centre; now it's time to use this to open up your higher heart.
- With power of Love and Light breathe in Cosmic Spirit from the Sun; acting as a conduit, magnify this in your Light centre, and send it to Earth.
- As Earth returns this to you in gratitude, instead of just a Sun and Moon sphere, the six spheres of the Flower of Life pattern will form in your heart; know they are there.
- Now, with the power of Love and Light ask the angels to help you breathe in turn the healing power of Breath of Life, Fire of Life and Water of Life.
- As you do so, heal these with the Flower of Life and again, with your heart as the conduit, send them back to Earth, Sun, Stars and all sentient life.
- It is this gesture that will open the magenta lily of your higher heart. You will feel pure Bliss, for it is the gratitude not only of Earth, Sun and Stars but also of the angels themselves that aids you.
- Your spiritual consciousness is now at One with All. You have truly found the Way.

Notes

Table of sacred seven and three

🖋 *The Way of Love and Light is through hope, courage, truth, wisdom, beauty, harmony and healing; it is a magical journey of transformation, leading to inner tranquillity*

Planet	Ruler	Day of the Week	Metal	Attribute	Key Symbols
Moon	Gabrielle	Monday	Silver	Hope	Moon sphere and crescent, five-pointed star, fleur de lys
Mars	Camael	Tuesday	Iron	Courage	Cube, square, red flame, earth
Mercury	Michael	Wednesday	Mercury (as in mirrors)	Truth	Feather, octahedron, butterfly, sword
Jupiter	Zadkiel	Thursday	Tin (Tin/lead as in pewter)	Wisdom	Nautilus shell, ouroboros, hexagon, Seven Pillars of Wisdom, Wisdom eye
Venus	Haniel	Friday	Copper	Beauty	Five-pointed star, Flower of Life, pink water lily or lotus flower and green lily leaf
Saturn	Cassiel	Saturday	Lead (Lead/tin as in pewter)	Harmony	Olive tree, snow flake obsidian, black and white agate
Sun	Raphael	Sunday	Yellow gold	Healing	Sun sphere, pyramid, tetrahedron, ankh, fleur de lys, clear quartz
Pluto	Ariel	None	Lithium	Magic	Six-pointed star, five-pointed star, violet flame, vesica piscis, amethyst
Uranus	Uriel	None	Iridium	Transformation	Fire pyramid (up), tetrahedron, amber, topaz, salamander
Neptune	Phuel	None	Platinum	Tranquillity	Water pyramid (down), icosahedron, aquamarine, malachite, water lily

Seven ⟵⟶

Three ⟵⟶

The rainbow chakra energy centres and correspondences

🖋 *Angels to help to correct the pure harmonic within*

Name/Location	Colour/crystals	Planet(s)	Flower	Ruling Angel & Qualities	Chakra issues you can address
Lower Self:					
Base/Root	**Red**: Ruby, garnet, red carnelian, red agate	Mars and Earth	Red rose	Camael: Courage, justice, energy, empowerment	Survival issues, worry over basic life necessities, security, grounding, low energy levels, confidence, bowel disorders
Sacral/Solar	**Orange**: Amber, topaz, orange carnelian, calcite	Uranus	Orange tiger lily	Uriel: Transformation creativity, sexuality, innovation	Sexual and/or menstrual issues, fear of life changes, writer's block, poor circulation, digestive disorders, urinary problems
Solar	**Yellow, gold**: Quartz, citrine, gold calcite, diamond	Sun	Sunflower	Raphael/Hermes Trismegistos: Healing, true power of will and intent, masculine balance	Shock or stress-related digestive disorders affecting stomach, kidneys or liver, lack of self-control, back pain, panic attacks
Heart and Thymus					
Personal Heart	**Green, turquoise, silver**: Malachite, green calcite, jade, aquamarine, selenite, moonstone	Moon, Neptune	Water lily leaf and closed bud	Haniel/Phuel/Gabriel: Healing personal heart with Water of Life, tranquillity, feminine balance, Ambition	Fear of relationships (past rejection), lack of self-belief/self-love, judging self too harshly, chest or heart conditions, lung or respiratory issues, circulatory problems
Higher Self					
Throat	**Blue**: Sapphire, blue topaz, larimar, celestite, charoite	Mercury	Blue iris	Michael: Personal and DivineTruth, freedom to be true self, strength of all types	Throat conditions, loss of voice, upper arm or neck pains, backache, swollen glands, difficulty in communicating or expressing true feelings despite desire for change
Throat/Third Eye	**Indigo**: Lapis lazuli, sodalite, turquoise, Starstone, fluorite	Jupiter	Indigo pansy	Zadkiel: Wisdom, abundance, integrity, kindness	Sinus issues, deafness, allergies, earache, neuralgia, eczema, skin problems, lack of spiritual awareness or perception
Third Eye/Crown	**Purple, Violet**: Amethyst, sugilite, lepidolite	Pluto and Gateway to stars	Violet crocus	Ariel: (purple)/Melchisadec (violet) Spiritual and psychic development	Headaches, anxiety, insomnia, chronic tiredness, migraine, disconnection from All, a need for spiritual direction
Higher Heart of Unconditional Love	**Magenta** and **Emerald** together: Kunzite, rose quartz, emerald, tourmaline, alexandrite	Venus, Blue Star, Zodiac, All and Oneness	Magenta-pink water lily flower opens in your heart	Haniel and Pistis Sophia: Heart balance – opening your Angelic Light Centre, transformation through flowering of higher heart	The opening of the higher heart flower (the spiritual heart) takes place when your heart is in balance, you can feel non-judgemental love for All Life, including self and wish to help to heal All That Is

A–Z of guardianship qualities of angels and mystical animal guides appearing in the quest

A

Abundance – Zadkiel,
Alchemy – Hermes
   Trismegistos, Uriel, and
   Feathered Dragon of
   Revelation
Animals, tame – Hariel,
   wild -Thuriel.

B

Balance, between Earth
   and Air – Ariel
Balance to third eye –
   Raphael and Gabriel
   (Caduceus)
Beauty – Haniel

C

Calming emotions with
   Element of Water –
   Phuel
Challenges – Cassiel, Pistis
   Sophia
Cleansing with Element of
   Fire – Uriel
Confidence – Camael
Courage – Camael
Compassion – Haniel,
   Pistis Sophia

D

Dreams, ambition –
   Gabrielle
Dreams, understanding of
   – Star Bear of the Violet
   Night

E

Element of Air – Ariel
Element of Earth – Ariel
Element of Fire – Uriel
Element of Water – Phuel

Emotional balance – Phuel
Empowerment – Camael
Energy and wellbeing –
   Mumiah

F

Faith in self – Pistis
   Sophia
Faithfulness – Golden
   Shadow Hound of
   Heaven
Fearlessness with
   tenderness – She-
   Leopard of Divine Fire
   of Creation
Forgiveness – She-Leopard
   of Divine Fire of
   Creation
Flower secrets of chakra
   flowers – Achaiah

G

Grounding, through
   element of Earth – Ariel

H

Harmony – Cassiel
Healing, rainbow powers
   of – Raphael
Healing of sun – Raphael,
   Gazardiel, Solar Lion
   with Ankh of
   Everlasting Life
Heart, healing hurts –
   Haniel, Phuel
Heart's desire, true –
   Pagiel
Hidden talents – Dolphin
   with Pearl of Great Price
Hope – Gabrielle

L

Living your Truth –
   Michael
Lost Divine Self – Roshel
Love, including of self –
   Haniel
Love, power of, to solve
   all problems – Rikbiel
   and Chariot with Twin
   Horses
Loving relationships –
   Haniel
Loyalty and faithfulness –
   Golden Shadow Hound
   of Heaven

M

Magic i.e. psychic-spiritual
   development – Ariel
Moon power – Gabrielle,
   and Phuel for associated
   waters, e.g. tides
Mountains and peace –
   Rampel

N

Nature's secrets –
   Achaiah, Peacock
   crowned with Nature's
   Secrets

P

Passion. for life, sexuality,
   change – Nathaniel
Patience – Achaiah,
   Michael, Rampel
Peace – Cassiel,
   Melchisadec,
Protection – Michael
Psychic development with
   Element of Air – Ariel,
   Star Bear of the Violet
   Night

R

Rainbow healing –
   Raphael
Rainbows – Melchisadec

S

Secrets of Nature,
   Achaiah, Peacock
   crowned with Nature's
   Secrets
Self-belief – Haniel and
   Pistis Sophia
Self-reflection – Shadow
   Hound of Heaven
Serenity – Cassiel, and
   Swan of Transfiguration
Sexual passion – Nathaniel
Speaking your Truth –
   Michael
Spiritual alchemy –
   Hermes Trismegistos
Spiritual perception –
   Raguel
Spiritual fast-
   tracking/spiritual
   fulfilment – Melchisadec
Stars, re-writing Life
   Template – Pistis Sophia
Stars, route to Unity
   Consciousness –
   Thunderbird of the Blue
   Star Angels
Strength – Michael

T

Time – Eth
Tranquillity and inner
   peace – Phuel
Transfiguration – Swan of
   Transfiguration (through
   Power of Truth)
Transformation, mind,
   body, spirit – Uriel

Trees, roots, strength and
   energy of – Zuphlas
True self, finding –
   Ithuriel, Melchisadec
Truth – Michael, Raguel,
   White Horse of Divine
   Power (one of Rikbiel's
   Twin Horses), Swan of
   Transfiguration

W

Wellbeing and energy –
   Mumiah
Willpower – Raphael,
   Hermes Trismegistos,
   Gazardiel, Solar Lion
   with Ankh.
Wisdom – Zadkiel,
   Hermes Trismegistos,
   Indigo Horse of
   Divine Wisdom (one
   of Rikbiel's Twin
   Horses)